TEACHING
BEYOND
THE TIME
LINE

TEACHING BEYOND THE TIME LINE

Engaging Students in Thematic History

China Harvey
Lisa Herzig

Foreword by
Sarah-SoonLing Blackburn

HEINEMANN
Portsmouth, NH

Heinemann
145 Maplewood Avenue, Suite 300
Portsmouth, NH 03801
www.heinemann.com

The authors and publisher wish to thank those who have generously given permission to reprint borrowed material:

Page 43: Loewen, James. *Teaching What* Really *Happened.* © 2018 Teachers College Press.

Image credits appear on page 161.

Library of Congress Cataloging-in-Publication Data
Names: Harvey, China, author. | Herzig, Lisa, author.
Title: Teaching beyond the timeline : engaging students in thematic history
    / China Harvey and Lisa Herzig.
Description: Portsmouth, NH : Heinemann, 2024. | Includes bibliographical
    references.
Identifiers: LCCN 2023046324 | ISBN 9780325170749
Subjects: LCSH: United States—History—Study and teaching (Middle school)
    | United States—History—Study and teaching (Secondary) | Curriculum
    planning—United States.
Classification: LCC E175.8 .H38 2024 | DDC 973.007—dc23/eng/20231108
LC record available at https://lccn.loc.gov/2023046324

Acquisitions Editor: Heather Anderson
Production Editor: Victoria Merecki
Cover Designer: Suzanne Heiser
Text Designer and Typesetter: Shawn Girsberger
Manufacturing: Jaime Spaulding

Printed in the United States of America on acid-free paper

1 2 3 4 5 VP 28 27 26 25 24 PO 4500885821

To my beloved parents,
Janet and Allen Green,
who dedicated their lives to ensuring
their children got the education they never had.

—CHINA

To all my history teachers,
thank you for making history relevant and engaging for me.
I hope to return the favor with my part in this book!

—LISA

CONTENTS

Each Appendix is also available online.

To access:

1. Go to **http://hein.pub/BeyondTimeline-login**.
2. Log in with your username and password. If you do not already have an account with Heinemann, you will need to create an account.
3. On the Welcome page, choose "**Click here to register an Online Resource.**"
4. Register your product by entering the code **THEMATIC** (be sure to read and check the acknowledgment box under the keycode).
5. Once you have registered your product, it will appear alphabetically in your account list under "**My Online Resources.**"

Note: When returning to Heinemann.com to access your previously registered products, simply log in to your Heinemann account and click on "**View my registered Online Resources.**"

OR
▼

FOREWORD

WHEN I ASK EDUCATORS WHY WE LEARN HISTORY, most responses fall into one of two categories: we study the past to understand the present, and we study the past to make a better future. Most people say both. No one responds that we study the past to recall discrete facts about history in chronological order. So why do so many students continue to experience history instruction as a timeline?

Here is a deep memory. I received a C on a history test in tenth grade. Maybe it was a D, but I'm being kind to my fifteen-year-old self. I remember that the test was multiple choice. And I clearly remember one of the questions I missed: "What year was the Magna Carta issued?" I remember because my teacher, who was generally warm and cheerful, was palpably frustrated with us. I wasn't alone; most of the class had missed that question. He told us the year of the Magna Carta again. He wrote it on the board and instructed us to remember it. I'm sure that at some point in the preceding weeks he'd told us the what, why, and who of the Magna Carta, but the traditional, chronological approach to history instruction had now led to an overemphasis on the *when* of the Magna Carta. It was as if the only thing that mattered was our ability to situate this document in its place on the timeline of history.

A few weeks later, on the next unit test, the question about the year of the Magna Carta appeared again. And once again, I got it wrong. Once again, my teacher was upset. More of the class had gotten the question right on the second attempt, but a good number had still missed it. Our teacher repeated the information once more, we moved on to the next section of the timeline, and the question was repeated again a few weeks later. I don't remember how many times this pattern repeated, but I know for a fact that at the end of grade we were still being asked, and I still didn't know, that the Magna Carta was issued in 1215.

Many students experience history instruction as a set of events from the past to be memorized, in order, so that we can list off the names and dates and get a good grade. Some students do well in these settings, at least as measured by tests like the ones I took. Some students even thrive, their curiosity sparked to dig deeper on their own or as they pursue higher education. But many, like me, flounder. I love history—my organization produces history resources; I've written a history book!—but I did not love history *class*. How could I possibly motivate myself to care about the date of the Magna Carta when I hadn't been asked to remember why the Magna Carta matters to begin with?

Teaching Beyond the Timeline reframes the traditional approach to history instruction by foregrounding theme, purpose, and context over discrete fragments of information. This is not to say that names and dates don't matter. They do. But what use is a name if you don't know what the person did, how they lived, and their impact? What use is the Magna Carta equals 1215 if you don't know why the document was created and why it still resonates today? Teaching thematically allows students to make meaning and to draw connections between the past, the present, and the future. Teaching thematically transforms history from something to recall to something to explore with curiosity.

Effective history instruction opens space for questions. "What else happened?" "How did different people experience this same era?" "What stories have been told about this event? What stories have been left out? Why?" Teaching thematically prompts students to ask these questions not only of the materials they study in the classroom but also of the materials they encounter outside schools. And yet, as teachers, adopting new approaches to our craft can be daunting. It can be difficult to teach in ways that we, personally, might not have experienced as learners. It's hard to adopt new practices without clear models. *Teaching Beyond the Timeline* provides those models. What I appreciate most about this book is that it is a book *for* teachers, *by* teachers. It doesn't just say, "Hey, we should be connecting historical events to themes!" It offers practical steps, activities, and examples to support teachers through the process of transforming their history curriculum and instruction, from educators who have done it them-selves, evaluated the results, and honed their processes. It is empathetic to the realities and challenges of teaching, and it foregrounds students and their needs. *It returns the heart and purpose to the teaching and learning of history.*

Right now, as debates rage around which history should and shouldn't be taught, and why, and how, thematic instruction allows learners to analyze multiple sources, perspectives, and moments in time, and to draw conclu-sions. Thematic instruction allows students to engage with perspectives that have traditionally appeared in online sidebars, if at all. And, perhaps most importantly, thematic instruction can offer students a sense of belonging and agency that they might not have previously experienced in history class.

I felt wildly unmotivated to learn the year of the Magna Carta. But let's say my teacher had read this book and had introduced the Magna Carta as part of a theme like "Striving for Liberty and Equality." A despot who abused his powers and a people who wanted to do something about it? That would have been familiar to me. And how that resulting document did not confer equal protection to all segments of society? I would have recognized something of myself in that. I would have drawn connections to other moments in time and to my hopes for the future. And yes, I even would have remembered the date. I would have thought, "Wow, 1215 is a long time ago, and it is still relevant today." But I would have learned so much more, and I would have wanted to keep learning.

—Sarah-SoonLing Blackburn, Ed.D.
Deputy Director, Learning and Engagement | Learning for Justice

ACKNOWLEDGMENTS

FIRST, WE WANT TO THANK ALL OUR FORMER AND CURRENT STUDENTS who participated in our U.S. History: Themes courses. Without you, this book would not exist. We appreciate the trust you placed in us as we developed our thematic course and continue to refine it. The feedback you provided us along the way—letting us know when a lesson was a hit or a miss—and your willingness to dive into historical content that was less familiar to you inspired both of us every day. Your engagement in our classes helped us feel we were on the right track resolving the issues related to "doing school" and wondering why history really matters in the first place.

Thanks to the parent and guardian community of the Acalanes Union High School District for your support as we developed our thematic course. Allowing us to experiment with new ways of engaging your children in the learning of history is appreciated.

A special thank-you to all our peers and colleagues. Many of you piloted our lessons and bravely transitioned from a chronological approach to a thematic one as we emerged from the pandemic.

Thanks to the district team, Ryan Boyd, Lyenne Denny, Kim Fisher, Matt Sweeney, Allie Tarantino, and Haley Walsh, for joining this journey with us by sharing your own thematic units, projects, and lesson ideas. Thanks again to Allie, who as a first-year teacher was hired to be a collaborator with our cross-district team: your ideas and enthusiasm, as well as historical knowledge, inspired us two veteran teachers to take our vision to a new level. We appreciate your reading of our early manuscript and spot-on feedback. Our deepest gratitude to fellow teachers Eran DeSilva, Kajal Chowdhury, and Rob Siltanen for your insights and input on our manuscript.

This book would not be possible without the incredible work of our Heinemann team, especially our editors, Heather Anderson and Tessa Hathaway. Heather, you understood our vision from the beginning and were always such a positive, encouraging voice in this daunting process. Your feedback helped us translate our concept into a beautiful resource for educators. Tessa, your tireless efforts in acquiring the necessary artwork and permissions were make-or-break for our book. Both Heather and Tessa turned our team of two into a team of four, making the refinement of the book an even more joyful endeavor. To the entire team at Heinemann: Lynette Winegarner, Pam Bachorz, Erika Kane, Victoria Merecki, Cindy Black, Suzanne Heiser, Kevin Bertolero, and Kim Cahill, thank you for your hard work and dedication.

From Lisa

Immense love and gratitude to my friends and family, specifically my husband, Max, and my daughter, Sam. Both of you gave us feedback, support, and encouragement along the way. I hope I made you half as proud of me as I am of you both! Hugs and kisses to you!

Thanks to my partner in crime and "sister from another mister," China Harvey. Truly, this thematic course and this book would not have happened without you wanting to take a risk and to try teaching thematically during a pandemic and amid a racial reckoning in this country. To me, the meaning of a true friend is someone who can teach you something and nudge you outside your comfort zone; you have continuously done both! Honestly, I can think of no better person to collaborate with; you made summer breaks somehow even more delightful as we worked on the manuscript together!

I would also like to thank my own U.S. history teacher, Mr. Glen, for making the study of U.S. history my favorite class and for being one of the few to believe that I could go to college—I recall you made me take the PSAT exam, even though I did not study for it! To my college history professors, you helped me learn the craft of the historian, rekindling my love of the subject and convincing me that history teaching was my higher purpose.

From China

I would like to express my deepest gratitude to Lisa Herzig, my colleague, coauthor, and close friend. There is no other human on the planet I could have done this with! Writing a book, I'm sure, can be a solitary process. But with you, my partner, this work is the product of true collaboration. We shared more tears of laughter than of frustration along the way, and I am proud of what we have created.

I am forever indebted to the inspiring and innovative educators I have had the fortune of working alongside throughout my career. While I could name dozens, in particular I would like to thank Paul Fitzgerald, Ed Seelenbacher, Kelly Ginocchio, and Eric Demeulenaere. Rarely do I create a lesson plan where I am not guided by the eternal wisdom of one of you. To my sister, Maya Bettencourt. As the earliest reader of our initial drafts, you bravely told us when the manuscript was off base, redirecting us to stay focused on our vision.

Finally, I would like to thank my family. Chloe and Isla, you are the motivation behind everything I do. Thank you for cheering me on and celebrating every milestone throughout this process. To my husband, Matt. You believed in this book from the very beginning. I am so grateful for your never-ending love and support.

INTRODUCTION

Why Teach Thematically?

TEACHER: "IN FOURTEEN HUNDRED NINETY-TWO . . ."
Students: "Columbus sailed the ocean blue."

A typical U.S. history course might begin this way, with the teacher calling out a familiar phrase from the students' elementary education, and the students responding in rote fashion. As the course progresses, the teacher moves through the content chronologically, often starting with the colonial period and ending with the Cold War, centering presidential elections and wars as pivotal events. In early spring, as the class begins its study of the European and Pacific theaters of World War II, one young student in the front row raises their hand to regale the class with their limitless knowledge of WWII battlefield tactics while the rest of the class sits and wonders, "Why do I need to know this?"[1]

Before each unit exam, students file through stacks of flashcards with terms like *Louisiana Purchase*, *Emancipation Proclamation*, *the Great Depression*, and *Mutually Assured Destruction* in black marker on the front. History teachers, being the creative, inspiring professionals we are, try to counter this collective ennui by incorporating historical simulations, lively discussions, and provocative debates. These attempts at engagement might temporarily raise the level of student participation, but we are often disheartened to find that our students still struggle to see why the information we are teaching is something they should learn.

We believe a more fundamental shift in the way we teach history needs to occur for our students to be truly engaged and see how U.S. history is relevant to their own lives. A genuine interest in the subject can make students stronger learners—when they engage and see the relevance of events in the past, they think critically about it; their brains are ripe for skill development. Moving from simple rote memorization to requiring students to meaningfully connect historical concepts, people, and events using patterns of comparison, causation, and elements of continuity and change over time is more valuable and useful to them overall. After years of reflection, we abandoned our traditional, chronological approach in favor of teaching history thematically. We organized the course and each unit around central themes designed to capture students' interest

....
1   Note: Throughout this book, we will use the terms they/them/their as gender-neutral singular pronouns.

and ensure our curriculum was inclusive and relevant to all our diverse students, a challenge we found increasingly more difficult to overcome with a chronological approach. We have created this book to help teachers understand why teaching history thematically is beneficial for student learning and to guide you through the process of creating your own thematic history course.

Of course, there are some benefits to teaching history chronologically. Our students learn the arc of U.S. history. Moving from the American Revolution to the Civil War, from the American Industrial Revolution through two world wars, ending with the geopolitical conflicts of the Cold War and the era of globalization allows students to easily anchor events in time and place. Students can see the influence of one historical event on another. Progressing through the 1930s and 1940s chronologically, for example, helps students understand how the United States' industrial support of the Allied Powers during World War II pulled the United States from the depths of the Great Depression. Additionally, history textbooks support a chronological approach. We have yet to see a high school–level textbook organized around thematic units. If your school, district, or state has content standards you are required to cover, they are certainly arranged chronologically. Finally, history teachers such as yourselves were likely taught history chronologically. If you are a veteran teacher, you have probably been teaching chronologically your entire career—you have a familiarity and comfort level with this approach and may be nervous to try something new.

Despite these benefits, the traditional chronological approach to teaching history does not always facilitate engagement in the subject matter. History often becomes a string of dates, events, and names that students are required to memorize without much understanding of why they need to know that material or how it may be relevant to their lives today. Most events are given a cursory examination because the teacher feels the need to keep moving through the content to get through the course of study or content standards, leaving little time for the students to dive into topics of interest and explore pieces of history that they connect with. This lack of engagement can make it difficult for a teacher to help students develop skills of critical thinking, reading comprehension, and argumentative writing because the students simply do not have a connection to the material.

Additionally, a chronological approach does not foster a culturally relevant and inclusive classroom. Our students have witnessed a cultural reckoning. Social media, streaming documentaries, TV shows, podcasts, books, and news outlets are creating a greater awareness of the experiences of a much more diverse community. Yet in most history textbooks, the lives, experiences, and contributions of women, people of color, and members of the LGBTQIA+ community are given relatively little coverage, relegating them to the last few pages in each chapter or pulling them out of the dominant narrative entirely, with snippets of their experiences briefly described in separate blue or yellow boxes in the textbook margins. Textbooks tend to center the experiences of those with formal political power over grassroots activists throughout history, emphasizing the individual contributions of the former and generalizing the latter. But our students are diverse in culture, language, gender, ancestry, and economic background. They want, and deserve, to see themselves reflected in the history they are learning. They want to learn about those who have been left out of history textbooks, uncovering contributions of people like them. Even when current events are brought into the classroom, they are often given short shrift as teachers race through hundreds of years of historical content. Rarely are students able to make connections between past and present events in a chronological history class, resulting in a general lack of awareness of how *their* lives have been impacted by history.

Teaching history thematically, however, can be a much more engaging way to structure a course. When teachers are no longer confined by chronology, the study of history becomes less about memorizing seemingly random dates and events and more about tracing particular ideas and movements across periods of time. Rather than a brief mention of the passage of the Nineteenth Amendment in the midst of the WWI unit, leaving students to think women's suffrage just happened out of the blue, students can trace the roots of the suffrage movement from Abigail Adams' letters to her husband, John, during the revolutionary era, through the Seneca Falls Convention, the disputes over who had the right to vote after the Civil War, the picketing and hunger strikes in the early 1900s, to the eventual ratification of the amendment in 1920. Imagine how much more interested students will be when they have a fuller understanding of historical concepts and do not feel like they are just terms they need to memorize for a test. There remains a sense of chronological order here, only more selective and in accordance with a unifying theme. The relevance of this focus on women's suffrage can readily be engaged through current events as well. Have students consider efforts at voter suppression or the continued fight for economic equality today and how these efforts tie into the movement of women and their allies across the country's history. In addition, this deeper dive into the content also allows students more opportunities to practice the historical thinking skills we value in our courses: understanding contextualization, recognizing the cause-and-effect relationship between events, and identifying continuity and change over time. Students can think much more critically about the events we teach when they have a broader understanding of their place in history.

We instruct our students at a unique point in their lives, when they are exploring their own political values and beliefs and developing as civic-minded, passionate young adults. They are paying close attention to major world and U.S. events that are unfolding before them. They want to know *why* things are the way they are and *how* we got here. Teaching thematically facilitates the connection between past and present events as it gives teachers the flexibility to start in the modern era. Themes can be built around current events, making the present day the foundation for the course where students dive into the past to uncover how we got here, creating a much more relevant experience for our students. They can see how history impacts their world today, giving them a much greater appreciation for the study of history.

Additionally, a thematic approach is much more conducive to creating an inclusive classroom for all students. Rather than following the dominant narrative in the textbook, teachers can create themes that allow students to see themselves represented in the curriculum. If you have been teaching for some time, you have probably heard your students ask questions like: "How come we only learned about immigrants from European countries?" or "Weren't Native Americans enslaved also?" or "What happened to the people living in the territories the United States colonized?" Essentially, the "Why haven't we been taught about [fill in the blank]?" question is one that most history teachers wrangle with, especially if they stick closely to the textbook. The fill-in-the-blank piece usually refers to traditionally marginalized voices that have been left out of the classroom. A thematic approach allows the teacher to center the class around these voices, providing mirrors for students to see themselves reflected in the curriculum and windows through which students can learn about people with backgrounds different from their own.

> "The identified theme or concept serves as a lens to identify, analyze, redefine, test, and reassemble the relevant events to develop theories that will make it easier to understand new events."
>
> **JACK ZEVIN, professor of Social Studies Education at Queens College, 2000**

HISTORICAL THEMES DEEPEN STUDENT UNDERSTANDING

Engagement and relevance facilitate learning. Recent findings support the idea that teaching history thematically helps students understand the significance of the material they are learning. Rather than focusing on rote memorization, teachers can present content organized around a bigger thematic picture that can build complex connections or schema for deeper student understanding. It is important to have a solid foundation of historical knowledge, but the thematic approach is not contrary to that goal. In fact, providing a main idea in the form of a theme increases students' ability for recalling knowledge, developing questioning skills, and understanding causal relationships (Peters, Schubeck, and Hopkins 1995). ●

Not only does a thematic approach benefit students, it also makes our job as a teacher much more enjoyable. Teachers can create themes that draw upon their own interests, as well as their students' interests: art, economics, social justice, literature, sports. Bringing our own passions into the classroom keeps us engaged and helps bring history to life for our students. Students know when teachers are excited about what they teach, and that excitement is contagious. If we love what we are teaching, our students will be all in, ready to uncover the past with us.

How to Use This Book

In this book, we will take you along our journey as two educators who recognized that the traditional, chronological approach to teaching history was not the best way to serve our students. In response to this realization, we began to research models of how to teach history themat- ically to create a classroom that was more engaging, relevant, and inclu- sive than the way we were taught and the way we had been teaching for years. However, we quickly discovered a dearth of materials in explain- ing how to structure a thematic course. In a recent study of social studies teachers using social media to discuss the advantages and disadvantages of the different approaches, the most frequently cited disadvantage of teaching thematically was a lack of knowledge on how to structure this type of course. Teachers had difficulty "determining the content, themes, the order of themes, appropriate teaching methods and materi- als to use with this approach" (Turan 2020, 211). As we developed our own thematic course, we encountered these same challenges and had to build from the ground up with a lot of planning, research, and of course, trial and error. This book aims to provide the structure that you need to overcome these difficulties in setting up a thematic history course. We will trace through our efforts and share our decisions on organizing course content, the themes we selected, and the methods and materials we utilized.

As we experimented with this approach, we discovered firsthand some of the real benefits to a thematic course. We found that teaching history through themes more easily allowed us to bring the modern era into the classroom, helping our students finally understand why the study of history is such a vital part of their education. It also enabled us to examine the past from the lens of traditionally marginalized voices, incor- porating stories that have been omitted from most textbooks. Immediately we saw student engagement increase, resulting in higher performances on academic assessments than we had seen in the past. Our students became curious learners, asking insightful questions and diving into their own research on topics we were discussing in class. Because of the success we were seeing in our own classrooms, we wanted to share our approach with teachers who may be new to teaching history and not sure where to begin or veteran teachers, looking to change things up in their classroom as they are finding what they've done in the past may not be working as well with today's students. Our book is designed to guide you through a step-by-step process of creating your own thematic history course.

This book is meant to be both informational and a workbook, and it is intended for both busy precredentialed and veteran teachers. We want this workbook to be practical and to offer ideas for different comfort levels with change as you may want to make more moderate shifts or add a few elements of your own. We will present the full array of changes we implemented, how we did it, and why, but we will also offer some modifications so you can gradually transition to a thematic approach, or enhance it even more so if it is already under way. To get the most out of the book, you should have a pen in hand to reflect, jot down ideas, and begin your instructional design. We have structured the book as follows:

First, we will take you through the fundamentals of thematic teaching from the building blocks of a thematic course to avoiding pitfalls along the way. Chapter 1 will walk you through the essential ingredients you need to start creating your thematic course. We will provide you with a general structure of the thematic approach and discuss essential elements that will make your course engaging and relevant, including identifying your personal motivation, engaging students through current events, centering identity and inclusion, and using an inquiry-based approach.

After addressing the fundamentals, we will move into the design process. Here you will apply all the essential components you read about in Chapter 1. This is where you will get to build your thematic course through a series of carefully designed activities. You will start with creating your course and unit themes in Chapter 2 and developing big-picture questions that you and your students will revisit throughout the year. This chapter is about establishing the foundation for your course.

Chapter 3 will dive into designing your units. In this chapter we will examine how to begin each unit with a current event and how to incorporate chronology into a thematic unit. You will build a unit from one of your themes and big-picture questions, while integrating requisite content or state standards. We provide several templates for brainstorming the essential standards and mapping your thematic unit.

Of course, well-designed lessons are essential to any successful classroom. Chapter 4 gets into the practical details of daily lesson planning, including use of engaging primary and secondary source documents and ensuring your students are developing the essential skills needed to be good historians. We provide two sample lesson plans, one that focuses on a broad period of time (in Chapter 5) and one that addresses a narrower time period (in Chapter 6). We discuss the merits of each and provide you space to develop thematic lessons of your own.

In Chapter 7, we will discuss diverse ways to assess student understanding in a thematic course, including written unit exams, project-based evaluations, and culminating end-of-year assessments.

Additionally, we have included throughout the various chapters ways to troubleshoot potential hurdles that may arise when switching to a thematic approach, such as ways to incorporate required standards, address students' understanding of chronology, navigate community expectations, and modify existing lessons to transition to a thematic approach more easily. We have a few words of advice on how to turn these obstacles into opportunities for a more engaging and inclusive curriculum.

Finally, in the appendices and online resources, we have included copies of the planning tools you will encounter throughout the book to continue designing your thematic course, as well as examples of our thematic unit maps, lessons, and lesson plans that we reference. They are yours to use, modify, or share with your colleagues! By the time you are finished with this book, the plan for your thematic class will be well underway.

OUTLINING INGREDIENTS FOR A THEMATIC COURSE

In This Chapter, You Will:

- Learn the difference between a chronological and thematic approach
- Identify your personal motivation for developing a thematic course
- Come to understand the essential ingredients for a thematic course, including:
  - Engaging through current events
  - Centering identity and inclusion
  - Using an inquiry-based approach

BEFORE EMBARKING ON THE DESIGN PROCESS, it is important to have a solid understanding of what it means to teach history thematically.

We will demonstrate how thematic teaching can help you use these tools altogether in more powerful ways, so your students develop a deeper understanding of history and see its significance in their own lives.

The Thematic Concept

Whether you are a new teacher or have been teaching for many years, you are certainly familiar with a chronological approach to U.S. history. The teacher begins the course with a particular date and event early in history, such as Columbus' arrival in the New World in 1492, the establishment of the Jamestown colony in 1607, or the signing of the Declaration of Independence in 1776. The teacher then moves in order throughout history, hitting all the "major" events—American Revolution, Civil War and Reconstruction, the American Industrial Revolution, Spanish-American War, World War I, Great Depression and New Deal, World War II, and Cold War—up to the contemporary era. Figure 1.1 shows how this timeline approach might be structured over a school year. Each unit heading highlights the various major events in succinct periods of time, progressing from the past through the present.

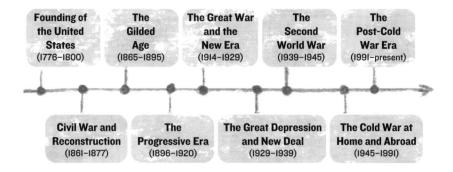

FIGURE 1.1 U.S. History Timeline with Chronological Units

This approach is easy to follow, simple to teach, and supported by your textbook's structure, but the march through history may leave teachers and students feeling like the goal is to simply "cover" U.S. history. A chronological approach does not provide students with many opportunities to make connections across time or really see beyond the dominant narrative to how history has impacted and been shaped by traditionally marginalized groups. A thematic history course, however, gives teachers the freedom to reorient historical time to create greater engagement and relevance for students. It structures units around central themes or ideas instead of specific periods of time. Each thematic unit would follow a chronological timeline, but the focus of the unit would be on the central *idea*, rather than the select period. In contrast to the timeline shown in Figure 1.1, a thematic course could be visualized as demonstrated in Figure 1.2.

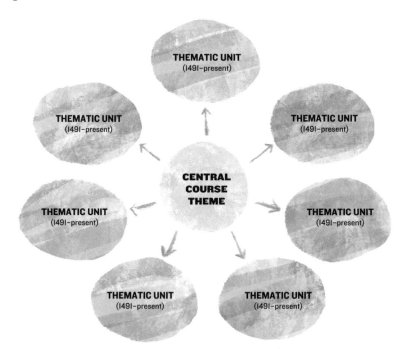

FIGURE 1.2 Template: U.S. History Timeline with Thematic Units

As you can see in Figure 1.2, there is a central course theme in the center with thematic units revolving around the central theme. In Chapter 2 we discuss in more detail the purpose and development process of central course and unit themes. But for now, consider the central theme as the foundation of your thematic course. It will frame the historical narrative you will provide your students with, tying all the curriculum together. Every thematic unit connects to the central theme, examining a particular aspect of that theme over time. If you think of your central theme as the hub of a wheel for your thematic class, the unit themes are the spokes, strengthening and supporting that central hub. Unlike the chronological approach, unit themes cycle through the historical timeline, examining different elements of U.S. history through a focused lens. This thematic approach gives students the opportunity to trace ideas in U.S. history over time, allowing students to understand how and why historical developments continued and changed over time and how those developments underpin what is happening in our present day.

This book will provide you with many examples of potential central course and unit themes you might use to design your thematic course, and you will have the flexibility to develop your own themes. But first, to help you further visualize what a thematic course could look like, see ours for an example (Figure 1.3).

Our central course theme, "Striving for Liberty and Equality," serves as the foundation for our entire course with each unit theme revolving around that central idea. Each thematic unit of our course spans the entirety of U.S. history, but because each unit is focused on a particular theme, students develop a much more solid understanding of that theme

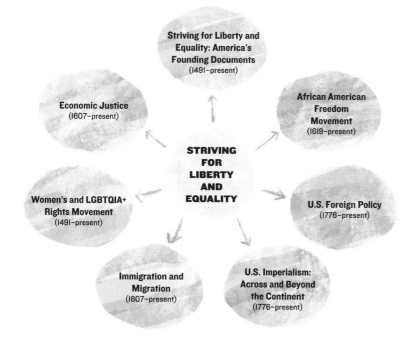

FIGURE I.3 U.S. History Timeline with Thematic Units

as they dive into it over a period of several weeks. For example, in the "Immigration and Migration" unit, students examine the broad history of internal as well as external movement of people from the founding of Jamestown through the present day. Throughout the unit, there are many opportunities for exploring the theme: students could identify patterns of migration, recognize similarities and differences in the experiences of various immigrant groups across time, and understand how centuries of immigration policy impacts immigrants in the United States today. Furthermore, this thematic approach allows students to revisit events multiple times over the school year, but through a different lens. Although some believe that repetition can be a drawback of teaching thematically, we have found that it helps reinforce students' understanding of the significance of an event or development. Students learn about World War II not only in the unit on U.S. foreign policy, but by studying the experiences of Black people, Native Americans, and women during the war and by exploring the impact the war had on the U.S. economy. By examining certain events in different lights, students will gain a more nuanced understanding of the intricacies and complexities of U.S. history than they would in a traditional chronological course that moves through the material in a more superficial way. Since each unit covers a broad timeline of U.S. history, the order in which you teach each unit is flexible; you can order them in a way that you think will be the most engaging and relevant to your students.

We hope this brief explanation of the structure of the thematic approach helps you visualize what a thematic class could look like. In the following chapters, we will go into much more detail on how to develop your own thematic course, including creating course and unit themes and designing lesson plans that support the thematic approach.

Essential Ingredients for a Thematic Course

Now that we have laid out the basic structure of a thematic course, let's look at what we have identified as essential elements to make that course both engaging and relevant to your students. Identifying your personal motivation, capturing students' interest with current events, centering identity and inclusion, and using an inquiry-based approach are all essential components for an engaging and relevant thematic history course. Although these ingredients may be utilized in a chronological course, they become fundamental with a thematic approach. These ingredients are baked into the thematic course, rather than served as mere add-ons or supplements.

Identifying Your Motivation

The first step on the journey of creating a thematic history course is to consider your motivations. Although we have laid out many of the benefits of teaching thematically, we think it is important that you take some time to identify why *you* want to create a thematic course. What advantages do you see for you and your students by teaching history through themes? What are some of the drawbacks to teaching chronologically? How did your experience as a student of history shape the way you teach, or want to teach, your students? How can your own interests help create a class that is engaging and relevant for your students? Identifying your personal motivation—what we call our "personal why"—will help you develop a rationale for the tough decisions you need to make on how to structure your course in ways that are best for you and for your students. It will also help you navigate some of the challenges you might face in developing and teaching your thematic course.

When we began creating our thematic course, we spent a lot of time in the planning stages discussing why we wanted to make the transition. Those discussions helped us determine the focus of our thematic course, particularly what we wanted our course and unit themes to be. As obstacles came up throughout the first year of teaching the course, we came back to our personal motivation to remind ourselves why teaching thematically was so important to us and why we believed it was in the best interest of our students. Although we genuinely believe that a thematic history course is beneficial for all students, creating and implementing one can be difficult. So we thought it would be helpful to share our personal why with you and give you an opportunity to reflect on why you want to teach thematically.

Lisa's Personal Why

Born in San Francisco, California, and raised by my maternal grandparents and divorced father, I am the first in my family to graduate from college. As a teenager, I was inspired by my eleventh-grade U.S. history teacher, who taught history through the experiences of ordinary people. He told the class his account of what it had been like to be a Black man in the Jim Crow South and in the San Francisco Bay Area, and he challenged his students to understand the complexities of the Vietnam War by bringing in a disabled veteran to share his story. I will always remember how this teacher brought the lesser known stories of America's history to life in the classroom. Often using the textbook as a foil, Mr. Glen encouraged students to interview family members and to make the past directly meaningful to our personal and family experiences. After interviewing my father, I learned about my family's Pennsylvania Dutch roots in the

Midwest and role in the early twentieth-century oil industry. After talking to my grandparents about their experiences during the Second World War, I learned how the wartime mobilization led my grandma to become a working mother and lifelong union member. These assignments from my U.S. history teacher helped me connect the history we were learning with my own families' experiences.

In college, I pursued courses in Native American history, women's history, and the modern Civil Rights era to find out more about subjects that were often overlooked in my early education. These courses set me on a path to pursue a major in history and then to become a teacher myself. As a new teacher, I was inspired by James W. Loewen's work, *Lies My Teacher Told Me*, to recognize and work around the dominant narrative in history textbooks and curriculum. Hired by the Acalanes Union High School District to teach U.S. history to eleventh-grade students at Campolindo High School in Moraga, California, I have continued to read history for pleasure and to improve my understanding of the complexities of America's history. As I began pursuing my master's degree in American history through the Pace-Gilder Lehrman Institute's program, I found access to inclusive resources to effectively bring college-level work into a thematic high school course. Working with like-minded souls in the district, I have collaborated with others on ways to make the U.S. history curriculum accessible to more students and to include diverse voices throughout the course.

China's Personal Why

Just like many of the students we teach, I did not grow up loving the study of history. In fact, history was my least favorite subject in school. The dates, the names, the events—they had no connection to me. I memorized the facts to do well on the tests, but as soon as the exam ended, all the historical information left my brain. It was not until my second semester of college, in an introductory U.S. history course, that I found my life's passion. My professor seamlessly integrated the contributions of women throughout history as part of the course. When discussing the American Revolution, the professor discussed women being the force behind the boycotts. When we moved into the antebellum period, the professor told us of the efforts of female abolitionists like Sojourner Truth and the Grimké sisters alongside Frederick Douglass. It hit me like a ton of bricks. *This* was why I had no interest in history before—I had not been able to see myself in it. With the inclusion of women, I had role models, roots, and relevance. I immediately switched my major from biology to history. As I delved further into the study of history, I found answers to other questions about my identity. As the daughter of a Mexican/Navajo father and a white mother who rarely spoke about their racial backgrounds, I was left in the dark about my ancestry. I wondered, where did my last (maiden) name "Green" come from? How is my dad Mexican if all his family is from Colorado? Why did my great-grandmother refuse to identify as Mexican, demanding she was Navajo, when everyone else in the family willingly calls themselves Mexican? Only through studying the history that was *not* in the textbook did the answers to these questions start to reveal themselves. The puzzle pieces of my identity began to take shape.

After completing my degree, I began teaching high school with the goal of creating a class in which all students could see themselves. The chronological approach to history through which I was taught in high school followed a white, male-dominated narrative—a narrative that barely even acknowledged the existence of people like me. Rather, I would uplift historically marginalized voices and show my students that they and their ancestors were just as significant as George Washington and Abraham Lincoln and Franklin Roosevelt. But year after year, state standards, antiquated textbooks, and district-approved courses of study got in my way, and I continued to fall woefully short of my goal. Finally, at a racial equity conference in New Orleans, I realized that to create the type of history course I honestly believed in, I had to scrap everything I had done and build the course from the ground up. After discussing with colleagues, my coauthor, Lisa Herzig, and I decided a thematic approach would lend itself to creating the engaging, relevant, and inclusive history course we hoped to instruct our students. Teaching thematically would give us more flexibility to ensure our students' diverse backgrounds were represented in our course and that we could connect the historical content to the present day, two important aspects of teaching history that are so difficult to achieve in a chronological course. We wanted our students actively engaged so they could practice the investigative and analytical skills of historians and see how our nation's history directly impacts them today.

Your Own Personal Why

Every one of our personal motivations influenced the course we developed. But this book is meant for *you*. In Figure 1.4, write down your personal why for wanting to develop a thematic course. As you reflect and write, consider these questions: What advantages do you see for you and your students by teaching thematically? What are some of the drawbacks to teaching history chronologically? How did your experience as a student of history shape the way you teach, or want to teach, your students? How can your own interests help create a class that is engaging and relevant for your students? If you are struggling to identify your personal why at this point, feel free to continue reading and working through the activities in this book. Your motivation might be clarified as you learn more about how a thematic course could benefit your students. Or if you are ready, take a few minutes to write down your personal why now.

OR 1

PLANNING TOOL: Your Personal Why

(blank lined form)

FIGURE I.4 Planning Tool: Your Personal Why

8   Teaching Beyond the Timeline

Engaging Through Current Events

One of the greatest benefits of teaching history thematically is that it facilitates students' ability to make connections to current events, which engages students' interest and helps them see how history is relevant to their own lives. History teachers often tell their students they need to understand history to understand the present. But rarely do history classes make meaningful connections between the past and the present. We all have the best of intentions to help our students see the links between the historical events we discuss in our class and the present day.

But with an ever-growing curriculum, that goal becomes less attainable as each year passes. On the other hand, our course must be relevant to our students for them to fully dive into the learning process. Engaging students through current events allows them to see what they are learning in your class is significant to their own lives.

Many history teachers do include current events as part of their class. Often, students are given an assignment where they must research and present a current issue. These can be very meaningful assignments, but often they have little or no connection to the historical content of that unit. Consider a change in the way current events are included in a history class. What if a particular current event was the *foundation* for the unit, and the historical content you chose to teach in that unit was meant to support students' understanding of the current event? For example, consider a potential thematic unit on who has had access to the democratic process throughout U.S. history. The unit could begin with a look at present-day voting laws. In the spring of 2021, the state of Georgia passed a law that many argued would result in widespread disenfranchisement of people of color. And it is not just Georgia. Since 2011, nearly every state in the country introduced a bill that would place more stringent regulations on who could vote (Brennan Center for Justice 2021). If you want your students to understand voting rights in the United States today, a topic they might be particularly interested in as soon-to-be voters, your unit might include an examination of advancements in voting rights such as the Fifteenth and Nineteenth Amendments and the Voting Rights Act of 1965. They could contrast these advancements with limitations some groups faced on their access to the franchise resulting from poll taxes, literacy tests, terrorism at the voting booths, and the 2013 Supreme Court decision of *Shelby County v. Holder*. Many of these topics would certainly be included in a typical U.S. history course. But imagine how engaged students will be if you *start* the unit with a topic that is relevant to them, then have them engage in inquiry to uncover the past behind these voting laws.

> "I understood why what we were learning about matters. It seems like a very simple reason that I discovered, but it was the first time I learned that history is not just so we know a bunch of stories, but so that we can know the context behind current events and issues, to get to the root of problems, and find out well-researched solutions. By having us relate back to the present, it answered questions about modern-day issues that I just assumed did not have answers."
>
> **Sandra** | student

A FEW RESOURCES FOR USING
CURRENT EVENTS

- Brown University's Choices Program, "Teaching with the News: Free Lessons Connect Your Classroom to Headlines in the News" (n.d.)
- Facing History & Ourselves, "Current Events in the Classroom" (n.d.)
- Larry Ferlazzo's "Seven Ways to Bring Current Events into the Classroom," Education Week (2020)
- AllSides

To make those connections clear, the teacher must be very intentional with the current events they choose to present and tie the events to the curriculum they are teaching. The sheer number of news outlets and potential current events to frame a unit can be overwhelming and make it difficult to decide which events to include as part of a bigger unit. To help facilitate this, we extensively use the "Teaching with the News" section of Brown University's Choices Program curriculum and the "Current Events in the Classroom" section of the Facing History & Ourselves website. Both sources regularly publish timely and relevant lessons that will help you bridge the gap between the historical content and present-day developments. They regularly highlight ideas about civic engagement, race, and gender, which can encourage thoughtful dialogue and engage students emotionally and ethically.

THEMATIC TEACHING IN ACTION:
Engaging Through Current Events

Here is an example of incorporating a current event at the start of a unit to engage student interest and curiosity (see Figures 1.5 and 1.6). In our unit on imperialism, we began by analyzing the current debate over Puerto Rican statehood. After evaluating arguments for and against statehood, students used a virtual whiteboard to share their relative knowledge and perspective on the issue. We included sample student posts on the whiteboard and the lesson highlighting the advantages and disadvantages of statehood for Puerto Rico. Once students were engaged in the present-day issue, they were much more invested in learning the historical background related to how the United States acquired the island, and more broadly U.S. imperialism and the Spanish-American War.

PUERTO RICO STATEHOOD: Pros and Cons

Directions: Read the short article "Will Statehood Benefit Puerto Rico?" Evaluate the pros and cons of this issue. As you read, list the important advantages and disadvantages to statehood in your own words.

Advantages:

+ There would be programs that would help Puerto Rico's economy, such as Medicaid, tax credits, and many more federal programs

+ Will have a stronger economic position; will increase tourism, entrepreneurship, and investment in business in Puerto Rico

+ Full representation in U.S. legislature and ability to vote on laws that affect the island; ability to vote on presidents

Disadvantages:

- Loses place in Olympics and Miss Universe; issue is independence of political status

- Could potentially lose multilingual tradition

- Tax structure may change

FIGURE I.5 Student Lesson: Puerto Rico Statehood *(continues)*

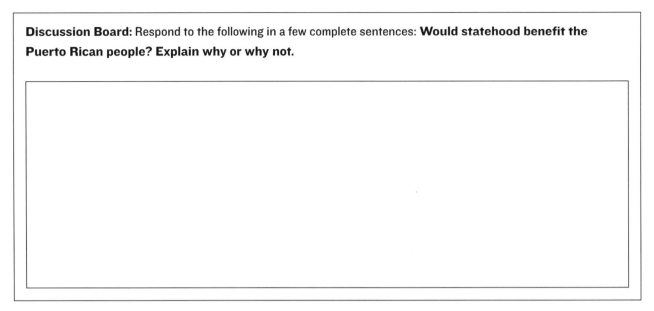

Discussion Board: Respond to the following in a few complete sentences: **Would statehood benefit the Puerto Rican people? Explain why or why not.**

FIGURE I.5 *(continued)* Student Lesson: Puerto Rico Statehood

FIGURE I.6 Student Responses to Question on Puerto Rican Statehood

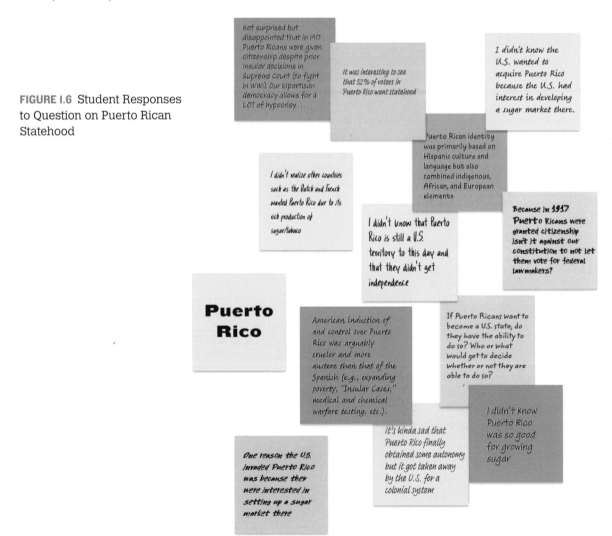

Centering Identity and Inclusion

To engage students in the learning process and make history relevant to their lived experiences, it is important to not only engage with current events but to center race and gender identity in your thematic course. The United States is a diverse country, and the study of its history should reflect this fact. History classes that focus on one narrative and that omit diverse perspectives not only are incomplete, but also often leave students feeling excluded and disconnected from the subject matter. Since the late 1960s and modern Civil Rights Movement, historians have researched more inclusive history and shifted away from writing "great men history." New subfields of history have emerged, such as women's history, Black history, and labor history, to examine the experiences of everyday people in the United States.

This scholarship affords teachers a vast array of resources to create a more accurate and inclusive telling of the nation's story. Now educators have access to many primary and secondary sources that present history from the viewpoint of diverse racial and gender identities. Even though these resources are readily available, the inclusion of diverse perspectives often does not take center stage in a traditional, chronologically ordered course. Part of the reason stems from the way teachers were taught history themselves, typically through the dominant narrative and in chronological order. Another culprit can be the ways history textbooks are structured, as most of these texts present history chronologically. If they include marginalized groups, they do so in a short paragraph—in a sidebar or at the end of the chapter—or as an illustration or graphic in one corner of the page. Although you could still incorporate diverse viewpoints in a chronological course, the thematic approach allows you to center these perspectives, bringing them out of the footnotes of history and into the full spotlight. Like those of European ancestry, the role of Black Americans, Asian and Pacific Islanders, Latino/a/x, women, and the LGBTQIA+ community are not incidental side stories; they are an integral part of the country's history and help make the United States what it is and what it has been. Thematically teaching U.S. history necessitates a cutting of the cord to the textbook's layout, an increased reliance on primary and secondary sources, and a true centering of race and gender to present a more accurate and inclusive story.

Many states are also recognizing the importance of teaching an inclusive history curriculum. In 2011, California legislators signed Senate Bill 48, known as the Fair, Accurate, Inclusive, and Respectful Education Act (FAIR Education Act), into law (California Code 2011). The FAIR Act

"[This] class was the first history course in which I felt historically included. Thus, I believe that the element of centering identity and inclusion is crucial. It is unarguable that unique ethnicities and races in the United States experienced history differently, therefore, why not include those different perspectives?"

Eric | student

compels that textbooks and curricula include the accomplishments of persons with disabilities, as well as lesbian, gay, bisexual, and transgender people. As of March 2021, five states in total (California, Colorado, Oregon, New Jersey, and Illinois) require schools to teach LGBT history (Aspegren 2021). As states increasingly move in this direction, thematic teaching provides an innovative solution of how to center identity and inclusion and still meet the course standards.

Although there is emphasis on creating inclusive courses, opportunities to bring in diverse racial and gender groups' experiences are limited in a traditional framework. Typically, textbook publishers will structure their books to mirror the chronological structure of the state standards and offer a paragraph or brief reference to major events involving women, people of color, and members of the LGBTQIA+ community, such as the Nineteenth Amendment, the Civil Rights Era of the 1950s and 1960s, and the Stonewall Riots, where members of the New York gay community protested police brutality. Textbooks present these events as examples of widespread forms of protest of eras, but they rarely make meaningful connections across time. Often, textbooks depict the Stonewall Riots as both the beginning and the culmination of LGBTQIA+ protests for greater political and legal rights. It is easy for students to walk away from the material believing this movement sprang from nowhere in particular! Students may not see the connections between this moment in 1969 and continued efforts to press for freedom and equality. Therefore, for students to better understand the patterns of continuity and change over time, restructuring the course to emphasize themes and allow students opportunities to examine primary and secondary source information can help teachers address these movements for equality in more relevant ways.

Because thematic teaching constructs units around central ideas rather than specific periods of time, it centers various aspects of people's identity more organically, resulting in a more engaging and relevant class for your students. As you determine which thematic units to include in your history courses (as you will do in Chapter 2), keep in mind the various aspects of identity, including race, gender identity and expression, ethnicity, and socioeconomic status. As we built our course, we centered many of our units around identity. You may choose that model or find ways to weave identity and inclusion in any thematic unit. Whichever model you adopt, it is important to acknowledge that issues of race and gender have been subordinated in the discussion or only briefly mentioned in textbooks and state standards. Thematic teaching provides an opportunity to bring these concepts to center stage. It can help engage students in more meaningful ways as they connect events of the past to more recent ones and see themselves in that history.

THEMATIC TEACHING IN ACTION:
Centering Identity and Inclusion

A unit on the industrial revolution does not seem to offer much on race and gender identity. You could teach the unit and avoid these concepts entirely by beginning with the causes of heavy industrialization following the American Civil War; the impact it had on living and working conditions, machine politics, and industrial leaders in the late nineteenth century; and the efforts of those trying to counteract these changes. This is a typical chronological approach. But if you created thematic units centering identity and inclusion, you might approach the Gilded Age in a way that is more relevant to your diverse student population. Although immigration from southern and eastern Europe is often included in the traditional approach to the industrial revolution, a thematic unit on immigration and migration could more readily incorporate diverse immigrant and migrant groups and could provide a more honest and inclusive account of this period. Examining Asian immigrants, who were also drawn to industrialized and urban areas of the United States, or the movement of Black migrants out of the Deep South and into Northern and Midwestern city centers would explore this period in greater depth and represent a more complete history of the late nineteenth and early twentieth centuries. Students could explore the reactions of native-born American citizens to these newcomers from within and without the United States leading to passage of the Chinese Exclusion Act in 1882, the national origins immigration quotas of the early 1920s, and increasing racial tensions. Furthermore, students could investigate the importance of groups like the Chinese in constructing the transcontinental railroad, the role of European immigrants in helping the United States emerge as a leading industrial power by 1900, and the efforts to create interracial alliances among organized labor and agrarian groups.

To further examine this period through a different lens, a thematic unit on women could investigate how the turn-of-the-century industrialization helped some women achieve financial independence from men, allowing them to cohabitate with other women in what were termed "Boston marriages," demonstrating a dramatic shift of gender norms. The same unit could look at the Supreme Court case *Muller v. Oregon* (1908), which limited the female workday to ten hours and established a precedent of protective laws for women based on inherent differences between the sexes. Although it is still important to examine the causes and effects of industrialization, the focus shifts from the role of elite political and business leaders and onto average people: how they changed and were changed by the forces of the industrial revolution in the late nineteenth and early twentieth centuries. With units that consider aspects of one's identity, teaching the Gilded Age moves from the traditional focus on captains of industry to how industrialization affected people, people like our students. Maintaining the rigor of the course content but making it more directly relevant to students is the goal in approaching this unit with race and gender at its center.

CENTERING IDENTITY AND INCLUSION WITH CULTURALLY RESPONSIVE TEACHING

In centering identity and inclusion in our classrooms, we based our approach on the tenets of culturally responsive teaching and learning. We have relied on the research of experts like Gloria Ladson-Billings, Geneva Gay, and Zaretta Hammond to inform our work. Their collective insight provided us with the foundational knowledge to transform our classrooms into ones that meet the diverse needs of our students.

Gloria Ladson-Billings (1995), a pioneer in the field, identifies three criteria on which culturally responsive pedagogy relies. The first criterion is academic success; teachers must evaluate and respond to students' academic needs to build their skills. She notes that the most successful culturally responsive classrooms were ones where teachers demanded, and students chose, academic excellence. The second criterion is that a student's cultural competence be maintained. Students' various cultural backgrounds should be brought into the classroom and used as building blocks for learning, not seen as something to "undo" in a student, as often happens in traditional classrooms. Finally, Ladson-Billings argues that a culturally responsive classroom instills a "critical consciousness" in students, empowering them to critique institutions, customs, and values that allow social inequities to persist.

In her book *Culturally Responsive Teaching: Theory, Research, and Practice*, Geneva Gay (2018) argues that traditional measures of student achievement expose systemic issues within educational institutions. Gay argues that culturally responsive teaching requires teachers to see cultural differences as assets, not hindrances. Bridges must be built between students' homes and the classroom. Ethnic and cultural diversity need to be integral to the content that is taught, whether the subject is social studies, math, English, science, music, or art. A strong class community and student-teacher relationships are vital to a culturally responsive classroom. Like Ladson-Billings, Gay believes students must feel empowered to challenge, critique, and change the status quo when it is not responsive to their diverse needs.

Zaretta Hammond (2015) examines the connection between brain-based learning and culturally responsive pedagogy, two concepts that until recently have been addressed only separately. In *Culturally Responsive Teaching and the Brain: Promoting Authentic Engagement and Rigor Among Culturally and*

Linguistically Diverse Students, Hammond explains what happens to the brain when it feels threatened, how it records memories of past experiences, and how it uses those memories to seek rewarding outcomes or avoid perceived threats in the future. If a student does not feel physically or emotionally safe in a classroom, their brain responds accordingly, going into "fight, flight, or freeze" mode. The brain cannot act in its fullest capacity, physically growing, so one can engage in more complex thinking and learning. As such, Hammond identifies four practice areas of culturally responsive teaching: awareness, learning partnerships, information processing, and community building. Culturally responsive teachers develop a sociopolitical awareness, recognizing the privileges and inequities one experiences based on race, gender, class, or language. They establish authentic connections with students, understand how culture impacts the brain's ability to process information and use that information to strengthen a student's intellectual capacity, and integrate cultural practices and curriculum into the classroom to create a socially and intellectually safe space for students. Hammond argues that culturally responsive teaching is one of our most powerful tools to close the achievement gap.

These scholars encourage teachers to expect academic success, to establish connections between home and school, to embrace cultural differences, and to create safe classroom environments. Centering identity and inclusion in our thematic units is one way to effectively create a classroom that better meets our students' diverse needs. ●

Using an Inquiry-Based Approach

In addition to using current events and centering identity, another way to help engage students with the content and connect the dots thematically is to use an inquiry-based approach, often by utilizing "big-picture" or "essential" questions. These are open-ended questions that can be posed to students at the start of a unit. They are intended to challenge students to think critically about the material in that unit rather than to simply test a student on their ability to recall the information. These questions encourage students to develop the skills of historians, asking them to make connections across time or geographic location or between distinct groups of people. Carefully crafted questions can help students make connections between the historical content they are studying and their own lives.

Although some traditional classes may use this inquiry-based approach to get at meaningful takeaways from a particular period of history, units centered around chronological periods of time are

"I've never seen history be taught this way, and yet this was by far the best history class I've taken. Having learned U.S. history chronologically previously . . . a thematic structure allowed for me to see connections between history and the present day, and come to conclusions independent of a textbook or teacher."

Makena | student

quite limited in their scope, making it difficult for students to understand the broader implications of the concepts discussed in a unit. By structuring units around more comprehensive themes, however, students could really practice historical thinking skills of identifying causation and continuity and change over time, including an understanding of how the concepts presented in the unit are relevant in the modern day. For instance, while examining the Great Depression and New Deal, teachers in a chronological course may emphasize historical developments and processes within the period 1929 through 1939. However, the thematic teacher could situate the Great Depression and New Deal policies in a broader context of U.S. economic history. A thematic unit could help students understand the critical causes and outcomes through various periods of economic turmoil, including those from the present day.

THEMATIC TEACHING IN ACTION:
Using an Inquiry-Based Approach

Let's contrast traditional big-picture questions in a chronologically format-ted course with potential questions in a thematic course. In a chronological course, the inquiry-based questions may remain focused on the late 1920s and 1930s. Students may be prompted to think critically and examine historical patterns, but the questions posed may remain tied to a very discrete period. See Figure 1.7 for some sample inquiry-based questions one might use in a traditional course.

BIG-PICTURE QUESTIONS: Chronological	
How and why did the Federal Reserve, Congress, and the presidential administrations of Herbert Hoover and Franklin Delano Roosevelt respond to the Great Depression?	How and why did the role of the federal government in the economy and U.S. society expand because of the New Deal?

FIGURE 1.7 Big-Picture Questions: Chronological

As these questions are based on a unit that only spans a decade, the familiar terrain of causes, course, and consequences are presented in very matter-of-fact ways. Students' responses to these questions will be extremely limited in their scope, and students may not be able to make connections between this period and those that came before or after. Certainly, students may point to the differences between the Hoover and Roosevelt administrations' efforts and the ways the New Deal took unprecedented steps to alleviate the misery of the Great Depression. However, we want to tap into broader patterns of continuity and change, and we also want to center race and gender in the discussion. In a thematic unit on economic justice, for example, students can trace the causes and consequences of financial policy throughout U.S. history, including its impact on women and people of color. Students could also examine the debates over the government's proper role in response to periods of unemployment, its attempts at redistributing wealth, and its evolving responsibility to ensure economic growth. This approach transcends the history of 1930s policies, so students can examine these patterns and debates now, making the lessons from the past more applicable to their lives. For students to make those connections, we offer two examples of what inquiry-based questions in a thematic course might look like (see Figure 1.8).

BIG-PICTURE QUESTIONS: Thematic

How and why did the federal government's role in economic disasters change between the late nineteenth century through the contemporary era?	How and why did economic recessions occur over time, and in what ways were women and people of color disproportionately impacted by these periods of high unemployment and economic fluctuations?

FIGURE 1.8 Big-Picture Questions: Thematic

In response to these two big-picture questions, we want students to understand the ways that industrialization created widespread wage and income gaps, particularly for incoming immigrant laborers. Students will also see the impact of unemployment and market fluctuations on women, such as the period after the Second World War and during the start of the COVID-19 pandemic, when the unemployment rates for women, particularly women of color, rose at disproportionate rates. Students could also compare the philosophies of the two major political parties regarding the proper role of the government in the economy during the turbulence of the late nineteenth century, the Great Depression, the 2008 recession, and the COVID-19-created economic crisis of 2020. These debates persisted even as the public grew more dependent on government assistance during times of high unemployment. The thematic approach, rather than a chronological one, can help facilitate students' understanding of these broader patterns across time. A longer view of U.S. financial history needs to be explored, beyond the era of the Great Depression—although this event would be a central part of a unit on economic policy. Approaching the content creatively with a central thematic concept at the heart of the organizational scheme can help teachers construct more effective, inquiry-based questions that tap into students' curiosity and engage them by bridging the past with the present.

Chapter in Review

Let's take a moment to review. In this chapter, we:

- Defined the differences between the chronological and thematic approaches to structuring a history course
- Gave our own personal whys and provided some space for you to reflect upon your motivations for crafting a thematic course
- Unpacked the foundational elements of thematic teaching that could make your history class more relevant and captivating for students by:
  - Engaging through current events
  - Centering race and gender identities
  - Utilizing an inquiry-based approach

FRAMING THE THEMATIC COURSE

In This Chapter, You Will:

- Create a central course theme and each unit-level theme
- Develop yearlong big-picture questions
- Produce focus questions for each unit

NOW THAT WE HAVE TAKEN SOME TIME TO REFLECT upon your motivations and provided an overview of the key ingredients, it is time to begin creating the course. Keep your personal motivation as well as those ingredients—incorporating current events, centering race and gender identities, and using an inquiry-based approach—in mind as you create the overarching theme.

Creating Central Course Themes

A necessary component of leadership is vision. Although this might sound like a topic discussed in a corporate retreat or when crafting a mission statement, vision is a valuable part of the classroom as well. Corporations or institutions that do not have a clear vision often become inequitable, lack accountability, and fail to possess a sense of shared values or purpose. Creating a central, course-long theme for a thematic course is important to embed vision to communicate course goals and provide transparency on how those goals will be met. The central theme also provides the basis of the historical narrative you want to impart to your students. A well-constructed and thoughtful theme can help anchor the course for students and for the teacher, providing a common thread through which the historical content will connect. Remember this image from Chapter 1 (see Figure 2.1)? Your central theme will be the hub of your course—all your unit themes will revolve around it.

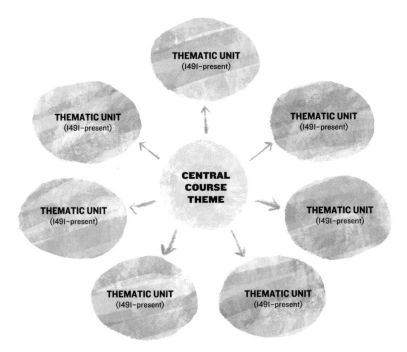

FIGURE 2.1 U.S. History Timeline with Thematic Units

The central theme should be thought-provoking and evocative. The theme should help students navigate the complexities of history and develop a more nuanced understanding of our nation's past. The theme should be relevant to students to fully engage them and help them see how this history connects to themselves and the present.

The central theme can be used throughout the school year in many ways. Your central theme will serve as a framework for each instructional unit. This will help you develop strong yearlong big-picture and unit-level focus questions. The central theme is also an invaluable guide for daily lesson planning. Truly, there is so much content to potentially cover that you really need to focus on the essentials; a well-designed course theme can assist in making the hard choices of what to emphasize and what to leave out. You cannot cover it all! A solid central theme can help you determine which resources, such as primary and secondary sources, videos, and textbook materials, to use within your lesson plans. The theme can be helpful in developing formative and summative assessments that reinforce course goals and objectives. The theme represents what it is you really want students to walk away with at the end of the school year.

THEMATIC TEACHING IN ACTION:
Creating Central Course Themes

When we chose our central theme, we considered our core values and reflected on what we wanted our students to get out of the course. We discussed our vision first. We believe students should see themselves reflected in the curriculum, and we want them to develop civic responsibility and see the value in being an active participant, all essential tenets of culturally responsive teaching. We also considered what was happening in the country at the time and thought about what would be most engaging and relevant to our students. As we were developing our thematic course, the Black Lives Matter movement was growing in strength and momentum, rights of the LGBTQIA+ community were being debated in state houses across the country, women were losing their jobs in disproportionate numbers because of the COVID-19 pandemic, immigrant children from Central and South America were being detained at the U.S.–Mexico border. At the same time, higher minimum wages were being passed and more women and people of color were being elected to federal and state legislatures. All these topics that were piquing our students' interests have deep roots in the history of the United States that were decades, or even centuries, in the making. Although they may be disparate topics, they all elicit questions of equality, liberty, freedom, and democracy, all fundamental principles of the United States. And they are all topics that are engaging and relevant to our students.

We knew we wanted present-day issues to be integral to our course, so we began brainstorming numerous central themes related to these topics. Looking at commonalities of each topic and how they each demonstrated both progress and regression for the groups involved, we initially chose "Struggle for Liberty and Equality" as our central theme. We wanted our students to explore the ways in which liberty and equality, two founding U.S. principles, have been fought for throughout history. However, we were dissatisfied with the word *struggle*. As lifelong learners of U.S. history ourselves, we were aware of the challenges Black Americans, women, immigrants, Native Americans, poor white Americans, and others have faced throughout the country's history. But we were also aware of the strength, heart, determination, and resilience of these groups. We did not want to portray historically marginalized groups merely as victims, but as agents of change who agitated, advocated, and demanded the United States embody its founding ideals. So, after deliberating, we finally settled on "*Striving* for Liberty and Equality" as our central theme. This theme allowed us to create a course where our students would examine the extent to which the democratic ideals put forth in the Declaration of Independence and the U.S. Constitution, the United States' founding documents, were accessible to all U.S. citizens. This theme could be traced across time and geographic location, through various demographic groups, up to the modern era. Our students could even apply this theme to themselves and reflect on the extent to which they have access to liberty and equality in the United States today.

We share our process because we hope it demonstrates the time and thought that we put into developing our central theme. Again, the course theme should provide a common thread through which students can trace historical events up to the present day. It will serve as the framework for each of your instructional units, and ideally, be woven into each assessment. Do not rush the process of deciding on your central theme. Ultimately, reflect on what you think is engaging and relevant to *your* students. But we encourage you to develop a theme that allows aspects of various cultures and identities to be integrated into your course, as we find that allows students to see themselves in the history they are studying, making the historical content more meaningful for them. Once you have a theme on paper, wordsmith it, sleep on it, get feedback from a colleague, revise it if necessary after you brainstorm some unit themes in the next step. In the end, you want to be confident that you have chosen a theme that will guide you and your students through a yearlong exploration of U.S. history.

Your Turn: Crafting Central Course Themes

Now that we have shared our process and our central theme, we will walk you through the steps to develop a strong course-long theme that will guide you and your students through a deeper understanding of U.S. history. If you have taught a U.S. history class before, consider some of the central ideas or questions that you and past students have returned to repeatedly.

CONSIDERATIONS FOR THEME DEVELOPMENT

* Past instructional questions or ideas
* An inspiring book you recently read
* Your state or district standards
* Current events
* Feedback from colleagues in the Social Sciences or English Departments
* Your personal interests or passions

Think big and consider broad concepts to explore. If you are new to teaching U.S. history, think about some of the recurring patterns that show up in the standards, in the textbook, and in your readings on the subject. Our central theme, "Striving for Liberty and Equality," was partly inspired by Danielle Allen's *Our Declaration: A Reading of the Declaration of Independence in Defense of Equality* (2015), which uses a close reading of the foundational document to reassert the importance of equality and liberty in U.S. democracy. A careful perusal of your state's history standards, familiarity with the textbook (if you have one), and a clear understanding of the instructional expectations in the district where you teach are all important considerations and sources of inspiration. It can also help to talk to colleagues in your English or Language Arts Department for some ideas. What texts do they use in their instruction? Do they examine any recurring themes during the course taught at the same grade level as your U.S. history course? For example, many of our district's English 3 teachers, who—like us—also instruct eleventh graders, like to explore the question of national identity and what it means to be a U.S. citizen. Remember that the course theme has many important purposes, so avoid veering too much toward the obscure or overly complicated when constructing it.

With that in mind, remember, only a word or short phrase is necessary, such as "Who Tells Your Story?" from *Hamilton: An American Musical* (Miranda, Lacamoire, and Chernow 2016), or lines from foundational documents like "A More Perfect Union" or "We the People." You might consider contrasting patterns or relationships like "Human Rights and Wrongs in United States History" or "U.S. History: Friends and Foes." You might want to select pivotal moments and highlight "The Ten Most Important Events in U.S. History" to explore. There are many ways to approach a course theme.

Now, let's get started by using the following graphic organizer to take notes as you explore various potential themes to use (see Figure 2.2).

PLANNING TOOL: Crafting a Central Theme

What topics have you found to be engaging for your students in the past? What are some current events that might be relevant to the curriculum and engaging for students?

What are you excited about in studying or teaching U.S. history? What are some of your interests or passions that you might incorporate into a course theme?

Are there any historical works that you have read recently that have made a big impression on your thinking? Look back at your personal why from Chapter I—what are some of your motivations for teaching thematically?

What words or phrases seem to recur in your state history standards? In your school's course of study? In your textbook? In your past course curriculum?

Have a conversation with a colleague in the Social Studies or English/Language Arts Department. What are some key themes they have used to explore their content with students?

FIGURE 2.2 Planning Tool: Crafting a Central Theme

Reflect on your responses to the prompts in Figure 2.2. What commonalities do you see? Are your responses pointing to a theme about politics and power? Human rights? History through art? Consider which ideas resonate most strongly with you. Now that you have created a large list of ideas that can be developed into a theme, you will want to refine and reflect upon them before making a final decision.

Now that you have a potential theme in mind, take some time to finalize it. Initially, we knew we wanted to explore the ideas of liberty and equality, but they did not make sense as just words at that point. Again, we settled on "Striving for Liberty and Equality" to complete our central theme because we wanted to emphasize how marginalized groups pressed for these founding ideals and continue to do so. Do a little wordsmithing, if necessary, to create something clear and accessible for students and yourself. Please record your final central theme in Figure 2.3 for reference.

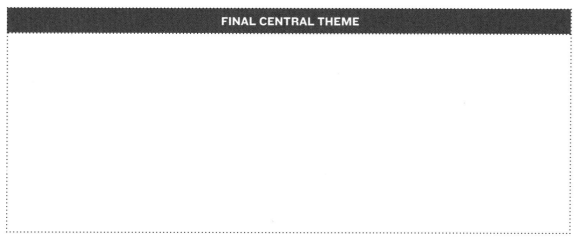

FIGURE 2.3 Final Central Theme

Developing Big-Picture Questions

The central theme you just created is integral to structuring your thematic course. Now let's turn to how we engage students with the theme through inquiry. It can be helpful to support the theme with one or two big-picture questions or prompts, sometimes called essential questions or guiding questions. The central theme and the big-picture questions work together to help students understand a larger idea and use an inquiry-based approach to exploring that central concept. Also, developing a big-picture question can help you and your students wrestle with the thematically organized content throughout the various units.

There are several important considerations when crafting that big-picture question. First, the question should be open-ended and subject to debate, without one correct answer. It should prompt critical thinking and evaluative thought. To make it even more engaging, the question should be provocative and incorporate your final theme into it. Consider asking a how or why question. You might also want to frame your question in the form of an evaluative prompt, such as "Evaluate the extent to which . . ." An evaluative prompt can help students access the gray areas of history, rather than a more simplistic black-or-white approach. Sometimes you may need to break the question into two parts to explore different historical thinking skills or ideas more carefully. Finally, the question should be useful throughout the entire course to help students take an inquiry-based approach to their learning.

THEMATIC TEACHING IN ACTION: Developing Big-Picture Questions

Using our theme of "Striving for Liberty and Equality," we created one big-picture question and one evaluative prompt that connected to our course theme and guided our students through the practice of historical inquiry. Our big-picture question and prompt are posted in the box below.

As we created the course units and questions, we directly referenced and often paraphrased the big-picture question and prompt. This helped us determine what we wanted to emphasize: the agency of marginalized groups of people and how effective efforts at "striving for liberty and equality" had been and are. We wanted our students to understand the importance of civic action and the role they all can play in continuing to strive for freedom and equality. We wanted our students to directly wrangle with the historical thinking skills of causation, contextualization, and continuity and change over time. Through the course, students should see the roles that courageous, every-day citizens played in lodging protests, organizing for change, and pressing those in power for a seat at the table. And they should comprehend how those efforts for change achieved some measure of success while others experienced setbacks or failed disas-trously. Students should understand how and why these various move-ments experienced relative success and failure and how later groups built upon the accomplishments, setbacks, and challenges of their predecessors. Students should realize that history is still being written and that they are an integral part of it.

Furthermore, the big-picture question sets the stage for formative and summative assessments. Each of our unit assessments connected the theme for that unit with our course theme. These assessments tasked students to select and marshal evidence to support their arguments about groups striving for liberty and equality and the relative effectiveness of these movements for change. Building on our goal of having students recognize the importance of taking direct civic action, one of our summative, end-of-year research projects required students to demonstrate their own effort to strive for greater liberty and equality (see Figure 2.4). We will delve more carefully into assessments and project-based learning in later chapters.

FIGURE 2.4 Poster created by Jay (Student), Addressing the Big-Picture Question in a Final, Summative Project

"My visual representation was made to represent the sacrifices made, the blood lost, and the work still needing to be done in order for everyone to have liberty and equality."

Jay | student

Your Turn: Crafting Big-Picture Questions

Now it is time to revisit the central theme that you selected and craft a big-picture question or prompt of your own (see Figure 2.5).

Putting It All Together

For ease of reference, transcribe your final course theme and big-picture question in Figure 2.6. In the next step, you will think about how this question or prompt can relate to potential unit themes, which we will model and you will develop. In other words, how might you explore this question throughout the entire school year in a variety of ways?

PLANNING TOOL: Crafting the Big-Picture Question

What is your central course theme?

EXPERIMENT: Write at least ONE "how" question.

EXPERIMENT: Construct at least ONE "why" question.

EXPERIMENT: Compose at least ONE "Evaluate the extent . . ." prompt.

Final Question(s) or Prompt(s)

FIGURE 2.5 Planning Tool: Crafting the Big-Picture Question

Final Draft of Central Theme and Big-Picture Questions(s) or Prompt(s)

YOUR FINAL DRAFT CENTRAL THEME

YOUR FINAL DRAFT BIG-PICTURE QUESTION(S) OR PROMPT(S)

FIGURE 2.6 Final Draft of Central Theme and Big-Picture Question(s) or Prompt(s)

Creating Unit-Level Themes

After you have devised your central theme and big-picture questions, it is time to create the various unit-level themes. The unit themes can guide you and your students through more specific content and support broader understandings of the central theme. Developing your unit themes is where you really get to start structuring the historical content so that it is more engaging, relevant, and inclusive for your students. You can create unit themes that you think will pique your students' interests and represent your students' diverse backgrounds. Devising your themes is where you can bring in your own interests and passions, while still adhering to state or district course standards. In this section, we will discuss strategies for developing your unit themes, share our process on how we developed our themes, and give you space to start brainstorming your own unit themes. After you have decided on your unit themes, you will start to see your thematic course take shape!

Your Turn: Crafting Unit-Level Themes

When choosing your unit themes, you want to make sure each one has a clear connection to your central course theme because your central theme will be the thread that ties each unit together. Your central theme may easily lend itself to unit themes. For example, if your central theme is "The Ten Most Important Events in U.S. History," simply choose ten events that you think represent pivotal moments in the country's history. But if your central theme is "Who Tells Your Story?" from *Hamilton: An American Musical* (Miranda, Lacamoire, and Chernow 2016), you may need to be more creative and thoughtful in choosing unit themes that connect to your course theme. If you know the musical as well as we do, you may be thinking of "Schuyler Sisters" as a title for a unit on U.S. women, or "Cabinet Battle #1" to create a unit on economic policies, including slavery. For a course theme on "History Through Art," you might select symbolic pieces of art, poetry, and literature to frame each unit. Langston Hughes' poem "Let America Be America Again" could serve as the foundation for a unit on the inclusion or exclusion of traditionally marginalized groups in U.S. history. Dorothea Lange's iconic "Migrant Mother" photograph could be the anchor for a unit on migration or women or economic justice in history. Again, if you think of your course theme as the hub of a wheel for your thematic class, the unit themes are the spokes, strengthening and supporting that central hub.

In addition to creating unit themes that are connected to your central theme, you want to make sure that each unit theme has enough depth so students can trace an arc throughout history. Let's say you settled on a central theme of "U.S. History: Friends and Foes." One potential unit theme could be "Alexander Hamilton and Thomas Jefferson." This unit theme would not only examine the relationship between these two U.S. leaders but could represent the broader vision of federal versus state power, an idea that can be traced throughout all U.S. history up to the present day. Similarly, a unit theme on Betty Friedan, a women's rights activist of the post-WWII era and author of *The Feminine Mystique*, and her nemesis Phyllis Schlafly, the conservative activist who successfully campaigned against the Equal Rights Amendment, would not only allow students to examine the second-wave feminism movement of the 1960s and 1970s, but could also serve as a jumping-off point for students to go back in time and explore the progress and regression of feminist movements of earlier generations, as well as look forward to contemporary movements for gender equality. If your central theme is "The Ten Most Important Events in U.S. History," a unit theme might be the "Wounded Knee Massacre." Here students could uncover the historical context both before and after the disastrous event between U.S. soldiers and members of the Lakota tribe to understand the centuries-long relationship between the U.S. government and various Indigenous Peoples. Whatever unit themes you choose, you will want each one to lend itself to an exploration of patterns of causation, contextualization, continuity, and change over time.

THEMATIC TEACHING IN ACTION: Creating Unit-Level Themes

It is also important to consider your own interests and knowledge base when choosing your unit themes. This was a key factor for us when we chose our unit themes. Our personal interests in women's history and the Civil Rights Era helped shape the unit themes we decided on. As we reflected on our central theme, "Striving for Liberty and Equality," and our own areas of interest, we found that the unit themes we brainstormed centered on the various identities within the United States and what went into forming them. Our initial list included the following:

* Striving for Liberty and Equality: The U.S. Foundational Documents
* The African American Freedom Rights Movement
* Immigration and Migration
* U.S. Imperialism: Across and Beyond the Continent
* Foreign Policy
* Women's and LGBTQIA+ Rights
* Federalism and States' Rights
* Economic Justice

There are so many ideas that did not make it to the final list, and we were certain from the start that the preceding list was still overly ambitious. It offered a suitable place to begin, but we still needed to fine-tune our unit themes.

After brainstorming the themes, we considered what students are expected to learn to ensure we were not forgetting anything important. We looked for patterns in the California History—Social Sciences standards to see how they matched up with our themes. Most of the themes we brainstormed worked out nicely; however, we discovered that "Federalism and States' Rights" might be a central theme itself, rather than a unit theme. Instead of using it as a unit theme, we chose to weave these principles throughout many of our other units. We believed we could discuss the ideas of federalism with the "Striving for Liberty and Equality: The U.S. Foundational Documents" introductory unit, and the notion of states' rights would be necessary to frame context for several of our other themes, especially the "African American Freedom Rights Movement" unit. We included Native American perspectives in our "U.S. Imperialism" theme since that was an area we both felt was important to discuss—even though there are few required content standards related to Indigenous Peoples. So our revised list of unit themes looked like this:

- Striving for Liberty and Equality: The U.S. Foundational Documents
- The African American Freedom Rights Movement
- Immigration and Migration
- U.S. Imperialism: Across and Beyond the Continent
- U.S. Foreign Policy
- Women's and LGBTQIA+ Rights
- Economic Justice

Again, we want our students to explore the concept of *identity* in all its myriad forms (race, ethnicity, class, religion, status, gender, and sexual identity, etc.) to understand our central theme of "Striving for Liberty and Equality." As we continue to teach the class, we anticipate that our unit themes will expand and evolve over time.

Now let's get started by using the graphic organizers in Figures 2.7 and 2.8 to take notes as you explore various unit themes to use.

If you answered no to any of the questions in Figure 2.8, consider reevaluating your course themes to further refine them. Remember that deciding on your unit themes is a process, and it may take multiple attempts to develop a course to fully reflect one's vision.

PLANNING TOOL: Crafting Unit-Level Themes

Look back at your central theme and focus question(s). What major ideas and events would students need to understand to explore the theme and address the focus question?

What are you excited about in studying or teaching U.S. history? What are some of your interests or passions that could be incorporated into unit themes?

Look at your state standards or district course of study. Think about the essential standards you want to address. What (or who) is missing? List these below. Consider how they can be incorporated into your unit themes.

From the lists above, select the TOP ideas. Most units range from three to five weeks, so consider how much time you will have for each unit—this might determine how many units you have time to teach. These will be your potential unit themes!

FIGURE 2.7 Planning Tool: Crafting Unit-Level Themes

Do you feel that the unit themes you created ...		
Connect well with your central theme?	____ YES	____ NO
Are culturally relevant and will engage students' interest?	____ YES	____ NO
Are inclusive of traditionally marginalized groups?	____ YES	____ NO
Have enough depth for students to trace patterns over time?	____ YES	____ NO
Meet the expectations of your district and/or state's standards?	____ YES	____ NO

FIGURE 2.8 Unit Themes Checklist

Developing Unit-Level Focus Questions

Now that you have created a list of potential unit-level themes, you will develop unit focus questions and prompts just like you did with your central theme. The unit theme works together with the unit focus questions and prompts to engage students through an inquiry-based approach. Like the big-picture question(s) you devised for your central theme, you should develop open-ended queries that have multiple interpretations and that prompt critical thought. With that said, it is wise to work smarter, not harder. Consider modifying your course-long big-picture question to fit the individual unit themes.

Take another look at our big-picture question and prompt related to our central theme:

* How have historically marginalized groups agitated, advocated, and demanded the United States embody its founding ideals of liberty and equality?
* Evaluate how various groups successfully attained their rights to liberty and equality.

THEMATIC TEACHING IN ACTION: Developing Unit-Level Focus Questions

For each unit-level focus question and prompt, we simply substituted and clarified the groups we identified in each unit theme. For example, consider our "U.S. Imperialism" unit, which includes various Indigenous Peoples as well as those residing in present or former U.S. territories, such as Puerto Rico, the Philippines, Alaska, and Hawaii. We subtly altered our big-picture question and prompt for the "U.S. Imperialism" unit like this:

* How have Native American peoples and those residing in U.S. territories agitated, advocated, and demanded the United States embody its founding ideals of liberty and equality?

❋ Evaluate the extent to which Native American and U.S. territorial peoples were successful in attaining their rights to liberty and equality.

As with our big-picture question, we want our students to recognize the agency of diverse peoples, evaluate the relative effectiveness of the various strategies and tactics employed by these groups, and practice the historical thinking skills of causation, contextualization, and continuity and change over time. These unit focus questions should have a replicable pattern and intentionally connect back to the big-picture question to assist students in gaining understanding of the central theme and how the smaller parts (the units) connect back to the larger idea.

Your Turn: Crafting Unit-Level Focus Questions

Now it is time to revisit the unit themes that you created and write focus questions or prompts of your own (see Figure 2.9).

Repeat these steps for each of the unit themes you developed. It is OK if there is some repetition to your unit focus questions and prompts or if they bear a startling resemblance to your big-picture question/prompts. Students will appreciate this and gain an improved understanding of the big theme and overarching question as you move through your various units. It can also be reassuring that you are on the right track with your unit themes if they connect to the central theme and questions in meaningful ways.

PLANNING TOOL: Crafting Unit-Level Focus Questions

What is your first unit theme?
EXPERIMENT: Write at least ONE "how" question.
EXPERIMENT: Construct at least ONE "why" question.
EXPERIMENT: Compose at least ONE "Evaluate the extent . . ." prompt.
Final Unit Focus Question(s) or Prompt(s)

FIGURE 2.9 Planning Tool: Crafting Unit-Level Focus Questions

Putting It All Together

Now that you have created your various unit themes and focus questions, record them in Figure 2.10 for future reference. Although there is space for up to ten units, you may have less than that number. We have seven content units and one block of time set aside for our final research project.

Chapter in Review

Let's take a moment to review. In this chapter, we:

- Discussed creating central course themes
- Modeled how to craft big-picture questions at the course level
- Highlighted various unit-level themes
- Demonstrated how to develop unit-level focus questions
- Provided you the space to produce your own central course and unit-level themes as well as corresponding big-picture and unit-level focus questions

Unit Theme and Unit Focus Question(s)/Prompt(s)

UNIT THEME	UNIT FOCUS QUESTION(S)/PROMPT(S)

FIGURE 2.10 Unit Theme and Unit Focus Question(s)/Prompt(s)

BUILDING A THEMATIC UNIT

AT THIS POINT, you have created the framework for your thematic class! In Chapter 2, you defined your course-long central theme and your unit themes. You also developed big-picture questions for your course and focus questions for each unit. In this chapter, we will go over how to construct a thematic unit, building from the unit-level focus questions you created in the previous chapter. You will also incorporate many of the ingredients from Chapter 1, including engaging through current events, centering inclusive content throughout your unit, and developing an inquiry-based approach by having students respond to your thematic questions. Through this chapter you will identify content standards and brainstorm essential content to incorporate into your units; you will map out the flow of your units to provide some chronological patterns for student understanding; and you will craft responses to your own unit-level focus questions.

Building Units Around Your Unit-Level Focus Questions

There are several steps involved in building a thematic unit. Since one of the essential ingredients for a thematic course is an inquiry-based approach, each unit will be structured around the unit-level focus questions developed in Chapter 2. Framing each unit around the focus questions allows you, the teacher, to determine which historical content and skills are necessary for students to understand as they address these questions. As we know, a teacher cannot "cover it all" in a yearlong history course. Narrowing in on the content students must understand to address your thematic questions is a necessary step when building your units. Consider the sidebar quote below by James Loewen, author of *Lies My Teacher Told Me* (2007).

As Loewen suggests, careful consideration should be given when determining the most essential content students should know. He does acknowledge that leaving out topics like the creation of the Constitution or the impact of the Civil War would be egregious omissions. But he argues teachers must be selective and teach content that connects to our students today. Using your focus questions as your guide should help you decide, even narrow, the content or topics you want students to understand.

While you are considering the essential content to include, keep in mind that many states require certain information to be taught. Some states provide content- and skill-based standards, and many districts develop their courses of study from these same standards. If your school or district does not require standards or possess a framework, it is still important to list the essentials of what students will need to know and learn from your course. As California teachers, to a substantial extent we must follow the content and skill standards the State's Department of Education has developed. We will be modeling the development of one unit of study from these standards. For our thematic unit on immigration and migration, we examined the California eleventh-grade content standards for U.S. history and selected those that would be essential for students to understand and use to address our unit-level focus questions. These standards are presented in chronological order, and since we are taking a thematic approach to the content, we had to make a list of priorities. Again, it is unrealistic to "cover it all" effectively.

> "Our goal must be to help students *uncover* the past rather than cover it. Instead of 'teaching the book,' teachers must develop a list of 30–50 topics *they* want to teach in their U.S. history course. Every topic should excite or at least interest them. What meaning might it have to students' lives?" (Loewen 2018, 23)
>
> James Loewen, *Teaching What Really Happened: How to Avoid the Tyranny of Textbooks* and *Get Students Excited About Doing History,* Second Edition (2018)

THEMATIC TEACHING IN ACTION:
Building Units Around Unit-Level Focus Questions

We will use the unit-level focus questions from our own course to walk you through this process. We developed unit-level focus questions for the "Immigration and Migration" theme, so let's use it as a model for construction. Our goal is to have students consider the historical reasoning skill of continuity and change over time, and we want to highlight the agency of international and domestic migrants throughout the unit. Our unit-level focus questions are provided in Figure 3.1. They are open-ended without one correct answer, and they offer us flexibility in how we approach the content. We have incorporated our course theme, "Striving for Liberty and Equality," in both focus questions, so it fits with our larger objective.

FIGURE 3.1 Unit-Level Focus Questions: "Immigration and Migration"

Diving into the Essential Standards and Content

To ensure students have the necessary content to address the unit-level focus questions, an important task is to reference our state and district standards and brainstorm the essential concepts, developments, people, court decisions, and other pertinent details we want to emphasize. If your school does not have state or district standards, then consider those details that would be necessary and important to address your questions from multiple perspectives. The California State Content Standards (California Department of Education 2000) address immigration and migration in several places. Since we have limited instructional time, we made some judgment calls on the most essential standards to emphasize. Though we are not teaching the course chronologically, the information will be organized in chronological order within the unit. Reviewing the standards can help shape the flow of the unit and organize it clearly for students who do not have a depth of knowledge of U.S. history yet.

After combing through the state standards, a good place to start the unit would be the late nineteenth-century American Industrial Revolution, enumerated in 11.2 in the California State Content Standards. From there, it would be essential to examine a few more key time periods when immigration and migration reflected key patterns of continuity and change, such as the early twentieth century Progressive Era (11.5), the Second World War (11.7 and 11.8), and the Cold War period (11.11). In Figure 3.2, the left-hand column lists the required content standards, and the right-hand column provides additional specifics not in the standards.

These specific developments to address would be necessary for students to understand within the highlighted time periods. For instance, legislation restricting Chinese immigration and the court challenges brought by Chinese people address both unit-level focus questions for the late nineteenth century: how immigration policy changed and how an affected migrant group addressed these changes that restricted access to liberty and equality. When brainstorming which developments to include, we considered what is required by the state of California *and* what is left out of our state standards. Oftentimes, state content standards represent a Eurocentric perspective. Centering identity and inclusion in a thematic course may mean a teacher must interpret their required standards more broadly to ensure multiple perspectives and histories are presented in their course.

PLANNING TOOL: Determining Essential Standards to Address Focus Questions

FOCUS QUESTIONS
To what extent has U.S. immigration policy afforded newcomers with rights to liberty and equality? How have migrants from Europe, Asia, Africa, and the Americas agitated, advocated, and demanded the United States to embody these founding ideals?

TOPICS/STANDARDS TO ADDRESS	SPECIFIC DEVELOPMENTS TO ADDRESS
✻ Industrialization and urbanization (CA II.2.2)	✻ Chinese Exclusion Act of 1882
✻ Push and pull factors (CA II.2)	✻ Geary Act of 1892
✻ Americanization movement (CA II.2.3)	✻ *United States v. Wong Kim Ark* (1898)
✻ Social Darwinism (CA II.2.7)	✻ *Ozawa v. United States* (1922)
✻ Anti-Catholic nativism (CA II.3.3)	✻ *Bhagat Singh Thind v. United States* (1923)
✻ Progressive Amendments XVIII and XIX (CA II.5.3 and II.5.4)	✻ "New Immigrants"
✻ Incarceration of the Japanese (CA II.7.5)	✻ Barred Zone Act (1917)
✻ The 442nd Regimental Combat Team (CA II.7.3)	✻ Emergency Quota Act (1921)
✻ Bracero Program (CA II.8.2)	✻ National Origins/Johnson Reed Act (1924)
✻ Hart–Celler Immigration Act (CA II.11.1)	✻ The Great Migration
✻ Frostbelt to Sunbelt migration (CA II.11.7)	✻ Fred Korematsu and Mitsuye Endo
	✻ Demographic shifts post–World War II

FIGURE 3.2 Unpacking the Immigration and Migration Standards

Now take a few moments and develop your own list of standards and essential concepts or developments to address in one of your units (see Figure 3.3). Select one thematic unit and focus question you developed in Chapter 2 and brainstorm what students would need to know to address it. As the James Loewen quote advises, consider historical content that is most essential for students to know, content that connects to their lives today.

INCORPORATING STATE STANDARDS IN A THEMATIC COURSE

It can be difficult to teach all required content through a chronological approach, and you might think there is no way to teach it in a thematic course. However, it is certainly possible to incorporate state and district standards with a thematic approach. It is not necessarily different material a teacher will cover, it will just be taught in a different order, arranged around conceptual ideas rather than segments of time as the guiding principle. And this restructuring of the content would allow students to make connections more easily across time, as well as making the course more interesting for your students!

To accomplish this restructuring, when we created our thematic course, we turned to our California state standards and our district course of study. We combed through all the standards to find those related to a particular thematic unit. For example, when designing our thematic unit on the African American Freedom Movement, we highlighted every standard that presented the experiences and contributions of Black Americans. These included a requirement to teach the American Civil War, short- and long-term effects of Reconstruction on Black Americans' access to political power, the experiences of Black Americans in both world wars, and of course their efforts in the Civil Rights Movement. Rather than teaching these in numerous units throughout the year, we simply sequenced them chronologically within one thematic unit.

At times, we felt our state standards were lacking in their coverage of certain key moments in Black American history, so we added greater contextualization with lessons on the slave trade, Black American agency in the abolitionist movement, and the effects of redlining on present-day communities. Although we took some liberties to enhance the unit and provide a more complete and inclusive picture of Black American history, we did so knowing we had closely followed the required standards.

If you are concerned a thematic approach will take you out of alignment with your content requirements, read your district's course of study or state standards. Use them as a guide to help you decide which lessons to create in each unit. Making sure your thematic course is tied to your district or state standards can be a source of comfort and familiarity and a way to ease the minds of administrators or parents who may be concerned your class is not aligned to your course of study. ●

PLANNING TOOL: Determining Essential Standards to Address Focus Questions

FOCUS QUESTIONS	
TOPICS/STANDARDS TO ADDRESS	**SPECIFIC DEVELOPMENTS TO ADDRESS**

FIGURE 3.3 Planning Tool: Determining Essential Standards to Address Focus Questions

Mapping Out the Flow of a Unit

After creating your list of standards and specific concepts or developments, it helps to visualize the flow of your unit. There are a few elements that you will want to include in the thematic unit, such as engaging through current events, providing the necessary historical context, and assessing students' learning.

For our thematic units, we like to begin at the "now" to help students understand the continuing relevance of history. It requires us to connect current happenings and events to our thematic topic. Typically, immigration is an often debated and sometimes polarizing topic. A new development, such as demographic information garnered from the Census Bureau, a news article highlighting the circumstances of those journeying to the United States, or a proposed piece of legislation could introduce students to why the topic is important and relevant to their lives.

After introducing a current event to engage students' thinking on the topic, we provide some essential information to help them navigate the thematic unit. This historical context may be a recap of the earlier historical events that affected U.S. immigration policy or internal migration. Since California requires that U.S. history be taught in the eleventh grade, it has been several years since students last learned U.S. history. In the eighth grade, students should have learned U.S. history through the Civil War and Reconstruction Eras; however, this is not always the case. We cannot assume (1) that students remember the information from the eighth grade or earlier, (2) that they were instructed or learned this material, or (3) that they were in a school that required this instruction. Students may have transferred from outside the state or even the country, so they may not have learned this information at all. It is important to level the playing field so all students can build their understanding from a similar point. In addition to some brief historical review or context, we may want to define some terminology to help students unpack information in the thematic unit. Some important terminology for students to understand in our "Immigration and Migration" unit would be "push" and "pull" factors, criteria for legal immigration, the naturalization process, and undocumented migration—to name a few. Addressing these key terms and concepts early on and reinforcing them throughout the unit is a good approach to help students dive into the content without being hampered by language or unfamiliar vocabulary.

Finally, it is important to consider the ways that you want to evaluate your students' understanding of the standards, thematic content, and skills. Although we will address assessments in a later chapter, it helps to set aside some time for these evaluations when plotting your unit. Also consider any project-based learning assignments that students will produce, as this may also require some time to accomplish.

THEMATIC TEACHING IN ACTION:
Mapping Out the Flow of a Unit

For our thematic unit on immigration and migration, we planned a four-week unit, which included a formal summative assessment at the end and an individual research project. Beginning with the "now," our introductory lesson would engage students in discussion on why immigration and migration are important. We would provide some historical context, briefly reviewing the movement of peoples from Europe, Africa, and Asia into North America since the late 1400s and up through the Civil War. The focus would be on industry growth in the late nineteenth century and the demands for labor that encouraged internal and international migration from around the world. We would also define some basic terminology, such as push and pull factors, to evaluate why people would leave their home countries and why they would journey to urban centers in the United States (and elsewhere).

When you map out the unit on the diagram in Figure 3.4, each box would represent a different lesson. Though the unit is centered around a particular theme, the lesson components are presented to students in chronological order. Each lesson component has been selected for its ability to respond to the unit focus questions. Students would analyze efforts to assimilate some newcomers and exclude others, the progressives' attempts to exert social control and dilute immigrant power through the franchise, the quota system, and the assumption that immigrants brought foreign radicalism. Since this unit also incorporates internal migration, students would examine the Great Migration, the movement of Black Americans from the Deep South into urban areas in the South, the Northeast, and later the West in search of new opportunities and as an escape from Jim Crow segregation and racial terror. Although not a voluntary movement, the incarceration of those of Japanese descent in the aftermath of the surprise attack on Pearl Harbor would also be examined, as well as efforts by Japanese Americans to challenge this policy through the courts and personal valor in the armed services. Even as Japanese Americans were being placed in detention centers, many volunteered to fight the Axis Powers in the Atlantic Theater. Similarly, Mexican Americans volunteered to serve in the armed forces, and the demand for laborers on the home front led to encouragement of Mexican labor migrations into the American Southwest under the Bracero Program. A transformative immigration policy came in the context of the Cold War with the Soviet Union: the Hart–Celler Immigration Act of 1965 ended the discriminatory quota system and gave preferences to spouses and children of U.S. citizens, those with professional and specialized skills, and refugees for entry into the United States. Students would evaluate the consequences of the 1965 immigration policy, which shaped the demographics of the United

States through the present day in terms of ethnicity, religion, language, and regional settlement. Throughout the unit, students would interview someone who immigrated to the United States to understand the personal impact of these policies and apply personalized context to present-day demographic changes.

As you can see in Figure 3.4, this thematic unit allows students to trace immigration patterns and policies over time, practicing skills of causation and continuity and change over time. In a traditional classroom, many of these topics would be included in the curriculum, but they would be given a cursory glance and would be spread out into several different units. Students would miss the opportunity to fully explore the history of immigration and migration in the United States and would miss the ways in which immigrants continuously fought to be included in the United States' founding ideals.

THEMATIC UNIT: Immigration and Migration

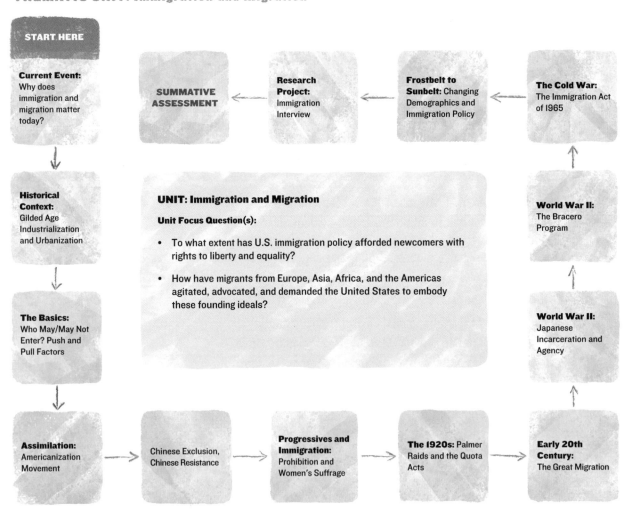

FIGURE 3.4 Planning Map for "Immigration and Migration" Thematic Unit

Now take a moment to develop your own unit map in response to your focus question, incorporating the standards and essential developments you brainstormed earlier. Consider a relevant current event to engage your students and the basic principles or terminology they would need to navigate the thematic unit. What would be the important historical context to provide to level the historical playing field for all students in the classroom? Figure 3.5 gives space for fourteen different lessons, but feel free to develop a unit map with as many or as few lessons as needed for each of your course units.

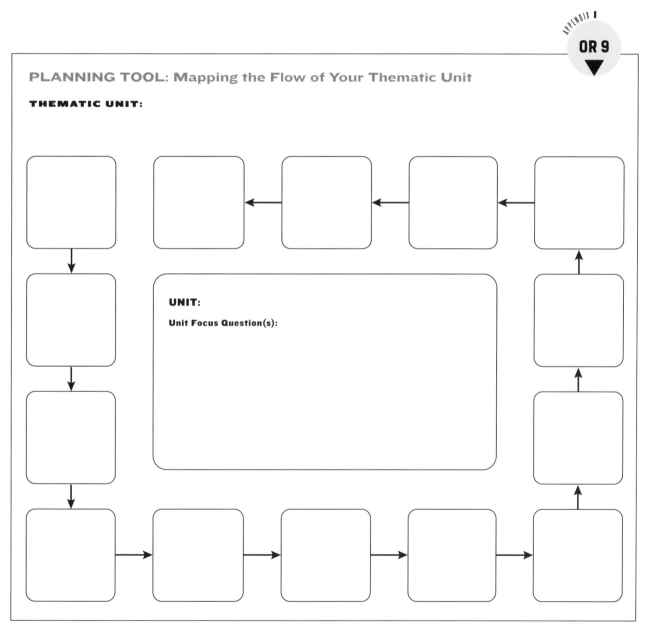

FIGURE 3.5 Planning Tool: Mapping the Flow of Your Thematic Unit

THE QUESTION OF CHRONOLOGY: HOW WILL STUDENTS LEARN THIS?

When developing our thematic course, we kept asking ourselves: How will students learn the arc of history if we don't teach chronologically? How will students understand the cause-and-effect relationship between certain events? How will they know how things changed over time? The question we should have been asking ourselves was: Do we believe that our past students *really* understood the chronology of history just because we taught it chronologically? We humbly acknowledge that the answer to this question is a big "no"! This helped us let go of the idea that history must be taught in a traditional, chronological way for students to understand it.

However, a thematic approach does not mean chronology is abandoned. Take another look at our unit map on immigration and migration. You can see that after starting in the present day to engage student interest, we go back in time and trace the history of immigration and migration in the United States chronologically from the nineteenth through the twenty-first century. We provide two more unit maps in Chapters 5 and 6, and you can see in both that we follow the unit theme chronologically throughout history. In our thematic class, we are teaching history chronologically, with a narrower focus to allow students to go deeper with each unit theme. In fact, we found that students have an even *better* grasp of chronology using the thematic approach because the course of U.S. history is covered multiple times during the year through a series of different lenses.

You may find it helpful to spend time at the beginning of the school year to present an overarching timeline of the major events your course will cover. Students can refer to this timeline as you move through each unit to identify how the events of the thematic unit fall within the scope of the broader timeline. Additionally, you can provide your unit maps to your students at the beginning of each unit. Your unit maps can become thematic timelines for your students to follow throughout each unit! Once again, this repetition of the historical timeline will result in an even stronger understanding of chronology for your students than in a traditional, chronologically ordered course. ●

Making It Personal for Students

When deciding which lessons to include in your unit map, make sure you are connecting the content to your students' lives in a relevant way. Although we will address crafting assessments, including project-based learning, more carefully in Chapter 7, these are principal elements in crafting a thematic unit and should not be an afterthought. Project-based learning can be a helpful tool for students to engage with the content on a more personal level. For this unit, we have envisioned an individual research project that requires students to interview somebody who immigrated to the United States. This is one way to make your thematic unit more meaningful to your students and can help students connect to many of the lesson ideas and standards. See Figure 3.6 for a sample of a student response to our immigration interview research project.

In this sample response, the student chose to interview his parents who migrated from India, highlighting the concept of assimilation through consumer products and popular culture. Other students interviewed friends and family from all over the world and shared historical events from the late nineteenth century through the present day. Students developed questions for those they interviewed that incorporated the thematic concepts of push and pull factors, patterns of immigration, assimilation, and the interviewees' perspectives on liberty and equality in the United States. Many of the projects highlighted the perceptions of greater economic opportunity in the United States and lack of these opportunities in other countries as factors for immigration. Also, many projects showcased new patterns of immigration after 1965, with an increase of migrants from Asia, Latin America, and parts of Central and Eastern Europe. Those interviewed attested to the socioeconomic benefits of living in the United States; however, they also pointed out the challenges of becoming a citizen

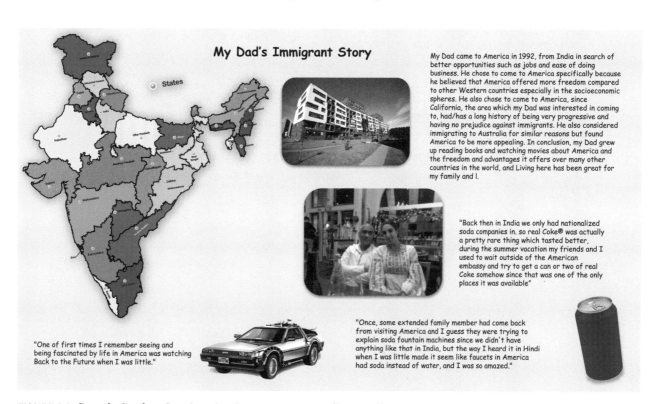

FIGURE 3.6 Sample Student Immigration Interview Project ("My Dad's Immigrant Story")

and realizing true economic equality. This project allowed students to connect the history learned with the experiences of people they know, essentially helping the events come to life. We explain the project in further detail, including student instructions, when we examine summative assessments in Chapter 7.

Crafting a Response to Your Unit Focus Question

Now that you have brainstormed essential standards and developments, mapped out the flow of your unit, and considered ways of connecting students to the historical content, you are well on your way to presenting a thematic unit to your students. However, there is one other step that can work as a double-check to help you filter the most essential components of the unit and establish a clear through line of analysis in your instruction: developing a thesis in response to your own thematic questions. You could even answer your focus question *before* mapping out your unit, but we prefer to do it after just to ensure our unit map covers our essential content and fits the time that we have allotted to the unit. See Figure 3.7 for our sample focus questions for our "Immigration and Migration" unit.

Taking the time to address your own questions can really help you figure out what is most essential for students to learn and to check the integrity of your unit-level queries. Answering our questions about changing immigration policy and ways migrants responded to these decisions, we wove the standards and brainstormed developments throughout our response. We have highlighted these legislative acts, court decisions, social movements, individuals, groups, and concepts to display them more carefully (see Figure 3.8).

UNIT: Immigration and Migration

Unit Focus Question(s):

- To what extent has U.S. immigration policy afforded newcomers with rights to liberty and equality?

- How have migrants from Europe, Asia, Africa, and the Americas agitated, advocated, and demanded the United States to embody these founding ideals?

FIGURE 3.7 Unit-Level Focus Questions: "Immigration and Migration"

As a result of **industrialization** and **urbanization** in the late nineteenth century, people from Southern and Eastern Europe as well as Asia migrated to the United States in search of economic opportunities and political freedom. These **push and pull factors** shaped immigration to and migration within the United States. Growing religious pluralism and ethnic diversity fueled nativist pressures to restrict migration for some (**1882 Chinese Exclusion Act** and **1892 Geary Act**) and to assimilate others (**Americanization movement**). Asian immigrants challenged these restrictions in court, resulting in acknowledgment of birthright citizenship (*United States v. Wong Kim Ark* [1898]) but also conflicting definitions of citizenship and equality (*Ozawa v. United States* [1922] and *United States v. Bhagat Singh Thind* [1923]). In the aftermath of the Great War and Russian Revolution, fears of labor radicalism and **Social Darwinist** notions about the "**new immigrants**" led to an increasingly restrictive federal immigration policy (**1917 Barred Zone Act, 1921 Emergency Quota Act**, and **1924 Johnson–Reed Act**). In addition, passage and ratification of the **Eighteenth** (Prohibition) and **Nineteenth** (Woman's Suffrage) **Amendments** were partly fueled by anti-immigrant sentiments. In the **Great Migration**, Black Americans moved to the North and West to escape segregation, racial violence, and limited economic opportunities in the South. During the Second World War, persons of Japanese descent were viewed as "enemy aliens" by Americans, even though two-thirds were American citizens. Many of these Nisei voluntarily served in highly decorated groups like the **442nd Regimental Combat Team** while their families remained **incarcerated** in remote camps through the war. Others, like **Fred Korematsu** and **Mitsuye Endo**, challenged the government's detainment in the courts. As many Americans engaged in a two-front war, Mexican migrant laborers fueled domestic agricultural work through the **Bracero Program**. In the wake of the Second World War and rising Cold War tensions, the Chinese Exclusion Act was repealed in 1943, and increasingly some Asian Americans faced new stereotyping as "model minorities." In 1965, the quota system was eliminated via the **Hart–Celler Act**, and this led to increased migration (both legal and undocumented) from Asia, Latin America, and Africa. As a result, the demographics of those residing in the United States have transformed ethnically and regionally with many moving out of the **Frostbelt** and settling in the **Sunbelt** during the postwar years.

FIGURE 3.8 Responding to Your Own Unit Focus Questions

- Erika Lee's *The Making of Asian America: A History* (2016)
- John Biewen's *Seeing White* podcast, "S2 E10: Citizen Thind" (2017)
- Roger Daniels' *Coming to America: A History of Immigration and Ethnicity in American Life* (2019)
- Densho Encyclopedia

Chapter in Review

Let's take a moment to review. In this chapter, we:

- Discussed building a thematic unit from a focus question you developed.
- Brainstormed concepts and events that would help students understand the chosen theme and that fit our state and district content standards
- Mapped out the flow of a unit, incorporating:
  - A current event to establish the relevance of the unit,
  - Some basic terminology to aid students' comprehension, and
  - Essential historical context to create a clear starting point as well as level the instructional playing field for learners with varied levels of content knowledge and exposure
- Addressed our focus question with a response that incorporates the various standards, individuals, groups, legislation, court decisions, and movements we brainstormed earlier

In the response in Figure 3.8, we have referenced many events that are not explicitly listed in the state content standards and may not be included in a traditional U.S. history textbook. We had to use supplemental resources to expand our content knowledge for the thematic units we chose. At left are some of the resources we used for our "Immigration and Migration" unit. We will sprinkle in a few more resources we used throughout the book and hope you find them helpful!

It is now your turn to address your own questions and reaffirm the concepts and developments you want students to examine throughout the unit. Pay attention to issues that arise, such as a concept, standard, or event that does not fit your theme or address the question completely. This might be a moment to reevaluate your question or consider placing the component somewhere else, in a different unit. As we developed our "Immigration and Migration" unit, our initial question was "To what extent have newcomers to the United States been considered 'Americans'?" We wanted to address the skill of continuity and change over time more carefully, and this question had some issues. First, it was difficult to address who did or did not consider the newcomers as Americans; this detracted from the sense of agency we wanted to explore. The original question also aligned a response along a spectrum of belonging, rather than rooting out the policy decisions behind these feelings. As we developed our thesis, it became clear that we wanted to highlight the changes of immigration policy over time and the responses from native-born as well as foreign-born people in the United States. As a result, we amended our question. Having a clear set of objectives spelled out can aid you in creating a sense of unity across your daily lesson plans and provide a clear determination for assessments throughout the unit as well as at its conclusion. Take a little time to craft your response to your own thematic question in Figure 3.9.

The next step is to continue working on your remaining thematic units. We have provided a few reproducible copies of the planning tools in the appendices and online resources to aid your development.

PLANNING TOOL: Responding to Your Own Thematic Focus Question

FOCUS QUESTION

YOUR RESPONSE TO THE THEMATIC QUESTION

FIGURE 3.9 Planning Tool: Responding to Your Own Thematic Focus Question

4

DESIGNING THEMATIC LESSONS

NOW THAT YOU HAVE MAPPED OUT THE FLOW OF YOUR UNITS, complete with focus questions, engaging current events, a general timeline of pacing, and a determination of the necessary historical content to teach those units, you are ready to start designing thematic lesson plans! As teachers, we know this is the heart of our work. A well-structured course is necessary for a successful class, but it is those day-to-day lessons when we get to implement that structure. This is when we engage with students, watch them make meaning of the material, and see the light bulb go off when a concept clicks for them.

The lessons you design for a thematic course might be similar to the lessons you would create for a chronological history course. However, unlike a chronological course that typically does not have a unifying theme, each lesson plan in your thematic course should be tied to your central course theme. After walking you through the elements of a thematic lesson plan, we introduce two approaches to lesson planning in a thematic course: one that spans a broad period (think: century) and one that focuses on a narrower time (think: year or decade). Both approaches will be modeled with examples from our classroom in Chapters 5 and 6.

When using either approach for a lesson plan, we want to encourage you to incorporate the essential "ingredients" that we discussed in Chapter 1: using an inquiry-based approach, engaging students through current events, and centering identity and inclusion. Just as you included these ingredients in your unit maps, incorporating them in your daily lessons will ensure that your thematic course is engaging and relevant for students, optimizing opportunities for learning. This chapter walks you through a lesson plan template that facilitates the inclusion of those ingredients into your lessons. Additionally, our template provides space for you to determine which historical content is necessary for each lesson, allows you to consider which type of sources would best support student learning, and helps you integrate historical thinking and literacy skills into the lessons to impart not only what students should know but how they should know it. And although our lesson plan template provides you with the structure to design thematic lessons that are engaging and relevant, it is important to keep in mind that there is no one right way to create a lesson plan! As teachers, we know that we need to use multiple instructional strategies to support different learning styles, and that is true whether teaching chronologically or thematically. In this chapter, we hope to provide you with inspiration and guidance as you build your thematic lesson plans, but know that there is room for flexibility and modifications as you design your own course.

How to Build a Thematic Lesson

Throughout this section, we discuss the various components of the thematic lesson plan using our lesson plan template (see Figure 4.1). This template incorporates many standard features but adds an inquiry-based approach and centers engagement and inclusion, important elements in a thematic lesson. Our template has three main sections: (1) space to develop inquiry-based questions and a lesson objective, (2) the basic elements of the thematic lesson, and (3) ways to assess student understanding and provide accommodation, so all learners can attain this understanding. We will spend some time walking you through each of these sections.

Again, in Chapters 5 and 6, we will dissect two of our lesson plans using this template. A blank template is provided at the end of each chapter for the broad and narrow time periods, as well as in Appendix K and the online resources, so you can create new lessons or adapt ones you already have.

CLASSROOM TOOL: Blank Lesson Plan Template

Lesson Title:	Time Required:

Unit Title:

Content Standard(s):

Course Big-Picture Question:

Unit-Level Focus Question:

Lesson Focus Question:

Learning Objective:

Historical Content	Instructional Strategy and Sources

Historical Thinking	Inclusion and Engagement Element

Assessment: How do you know that students have achieved the learning objective?

Modifications/Accommodations: How can you provide the necessary modifications or accommodations for special education/English language learner students to achieve the learning objective?

FIGURE 4.I Classroom Tool: Blank Lesson Plan Template

Inquiry-Based Approach

Just as we use inquiry-based questions at the course level (Chapter 2) and unit level (Chapter 3), we have found that centering lessons around a focus question allows students to use the skills of a historian and move away from lessons that focus on rote memorization. After completing the unit title and lesson name and calculating the time required for students to do the lesson, fill in the content standard(s) or specific historical developments that you want to address (see Figure 4.2). Remember that you had previously identified these standards and developments while creating your unit map.

CLASSROOM TOOL: Blank Lesson Plan Template

Lesson Title:	Time Required:
Unit Title:	
Content Standard(s):	
Course Big-Picture Question:	
Unit-Level Focus Question:	
Lesson Focus Question:	
Learning Objective:	

FIGURE 4.2 Lesson Template: Inquiry-Based Approach

THEMATIC TEACHING IN ACTION: An Inquiry-Based Approach

The inquiry questions you have created at the course and unit levels will be instrumental in developing your lesson focus questions. Let's recap our inquiry questions as an example. For our course theme, "Striving for Liberty and Equality," we use the following big-picture questions:

❖ How have historically marginalized groups agitated, advocated, and demanded the United States embody its founding ideals of liberty and equality?

❖ Evaluate how various groups successfully attained their rights to liberty and equality.

As much as possible, we derived our unit-level questions from our big-picture questions. In Chapter 3, we used our "Immigration and Migration" unit to demonstrate how we developed unit-level focus questions. As a reminder, the focus questions that frame that unit are:

* To what extent has U.S. immigration policy afforded newcomers with rights to liberty and equality?
* How have migrants from Europe, Asia, Africa, and the Americas agitated, advocated, and demanded the United States embody these founding ideals?

As you can see, the unit-level focus questions are pulled from the course big-picture questions—they are specific to a particular unit theme, in this case, "Immigration and Migration."

We use a similar formula when creating lesson-level focus questions. Take another look at the unit map for our "Immigration and Migration" unit from Chapter 3 (see Figure 4.3).

You can see the focus questions in the center and each lesson topic around the outside. For our lesson plan on the topic of Chinese exclusion and Chinese resistance, we considered our unit-level focus questions when deciding what inquiry we wanted our students to engage in for this lesson. Wanting students to demonstrate a strong understanding of the historical time, including the actions of the U.S. government and the effects of those actions, we settled on the following for our lesson focus question:

* Why was Chinese immigration restricted in 1882, and how did the restrictions affect this immigrant population?

By addressing this question, students are building a response to the broader unit-level questions, touching upon our theme of liberty and equality, and examining not only the various impacts the Chinese Exclusion Act had on Chinese immigrants, but also the various responses Chinese immigrants had to the act. Our goal with this step is to ensure some cohesion across our course from the individual lessons through unit themes to the broad big-picture questions that anchor the class.

The last step in this section of the lesson plan template is to identify a clear lesson objective. At this point, we have created a lesson that addresses the historical content and requires the use of one or more historical thinking skills. In the example lesson focus question, we identify Chinese exclusion as the historical content and require students to consider cause and effect as they interact with the course materials provided to them. We want students to develop their own conclusions about the lesson content using the skills of the historian. Therefore, a good lesson objective for this topic would be: students will address the learning

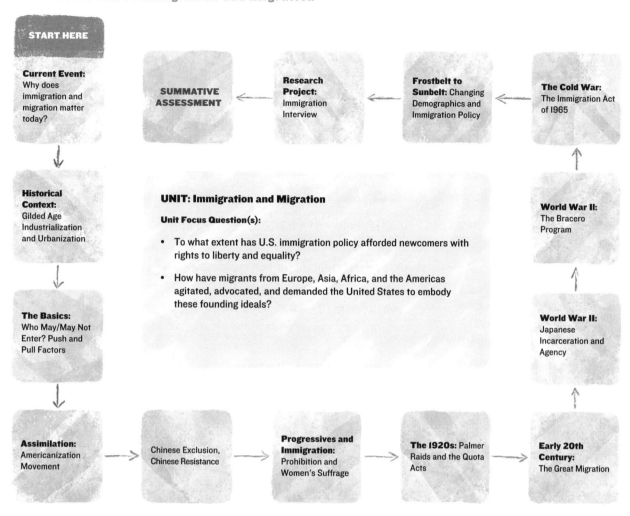

START HERE

Current Event: Why does immigration and migration matter today?

Historical Context: Gilded Age Industrialization and Urbanization

The Basics: Who May/May Not Enter? Push and Pull Factors

Assimilation: Americanization Movement

Chinese Exclusion, Chinese Resistance

Progressives and Immigration: Prohibition and Women's Suffrage

The 1920s: Palmer Raids and the Quota Acts

Early 20th Century: The Great Migration

SUMMATIVE ASSESSMENT

Research Project: Immigration Interview

Frostbelt to Sunbelt: Changing Demographics and Immigration Policy

The Cold War: The Immigration Act of 1965

World War II: The Bracero Program

World War II: Japanese Incarceration and Agency

UNIT: Immigration and Migration

Unit Focus Question(s):

- To what extent has U.S. immigration policy afforded newcomers with rights to liberty and equality?

- How have migrants from Europe, Asia, Africa, and the Americas agitated, advocated, and demanded the United States to embody these founding ideals?

FIGURE 4.3 Planning Map for "Immigration and Migration" Thematic Unit

focus question using historical content and the historical thinking skill of cause and effect. This simple objective incorporates both what you want your students to *know* and what you want them to be able to *do*. Furthermore, the lesson objective can make a great formative assessment at the end of the lesson, as we will discuss later in this chapter.

Elements of the Thematic Lesson

The second section of our thematic lesson plan template that we will examine covers the components of a thematic lesson: historical content, historical thinking, instructional strategies and sources, and elements of inclusion and engagement. Consider this section the *how* of your lesson—*How* are you going to structure your lesson so students can achieve the lesson objective? These elements may be familiar to you, especially if you have been teaching for years. In this section, we will show you how we have incorporated these lesson ingredients to fit our thematic approach.

Historical Content	Instructional Strategy and Sources
Historical Thinking	Inclusion and Engagement Element

FIGURE 4.4 Lesson Template: Elements of the Thematic Lesson

After settling on a lesson focus question, the next step is determining what historical content students need to know to answer it. Like the process you went through when evaluating essential standards and developments in Chapter 3, use this space on the lesson plan template to jot down a list of historical events, people, laws, ideas, and so on. This will serve as the evidence your students will use when answering the lesson focus question. If you are required to teach specific content by your state or district, this step will help ensure you are meeting that requirement. It is also important to consider the necessary historical context students will need to understand the content of this lesson. This is especially true for a thematic course since we are potentially providing a lesson spanning more than a century's worth of content. This context should provide an entryway to the historical content and be supportive of the content standard(s) you identified at the top of your lesson plan.

Next, it is important to determine which *historical thinking* skill you are asking your students to utilize when answering the lesson focus question. Is your question asking students to consider the cause-and-effect relationship between events? The extent to which ideas or developments changed over time? Similarities and differences between two historical events? Our question for our "Chinese Exclusion, Chinese Resistance" lesson requires students to use the historical thinking skill of cause and effect: Why was Chinese immigration restricted in 1882 [cause], and how did the restrictions affect this immigrant population [effect]? If you cannot easily identify which skill you are assessing, your inquiry question might be too close-ended, requiring students to supply one correct answer or a simple yes-or-no response. Lesson focus questions should elicit multiple correct responses. Just as historians have different interpretations of historical events, we want our students to make their own arguments with the historical evidence provided to them.

"Textbooks and lectures, by themselves, cannot easily communicate such thoughts and experiences, and even the most eloquent historians include quotations from original sources throughout their works. By carefully reading these sources and considering their meaning, we reach our own conclusions about how people in the past experienced their lives. In this way, original sources are used not just to establish the existence of historical trends and events but to provide insight into the meaning they held for people who lived through them." (2005, 753)

Keith C. Barton, *Phi Delta Kappan* (Vol. 86, No. 10), p. 753, copyright © 2005 by SAGE Publications. Reprinted by permission of SAGE Publications.

Keith C. Barton, history professor in the Department of Curriculum and Instruction at Indiana University, Bloomington

Once you have identified the historical content and skills required in your lesson, the next step is to determine which *instructional strategy and sources* would be best to teach the lesson. As we have noted, one of the benefits of teaching thematically is that the focus is on student understanding of a *concept* rather than simply memorizing historical facts. With that in mind, the instructional strategies you choose should facilitate that understanding. A brief lecture might be appropriate for providing historical context, but then consider instructional strategies that put students in the role of historian. Analyzing primary and secondary sources, engaging in historical discussion, and building reading and writing skills all allow students to engage with the material in a deeper way and provide them the support they will need to answer the lesson focus question and solidify greater understanding of the content. Look at the chart in Figure 4.5 for some examples of these strategies.

COMMON SOCIAL STUDIES INSTRUCTIONAL STRATEGIES

Source Analysis Strategies	Writing Strategies	Discussion Strategies
* Analyzing Images * Document Analysis: HAPPY (Historical Context, Audience, Purpose, and Point of View) * Gallery Walk * News Article Analysis * Secondary Source Analysis (Historical Interpretation) * Video Analysis	* Annotating or Paraphrasing Text * Close Reading Strategy * Concept Mapping * Dissecting a Prompt * Evidence Logs (Graphic Organizers) * Exit Tickets * Journaling * K-W-L (What I Know, What I Want to Know, What I Learned) Charts * S-I-T (Surprising, Interesting, Troubling)	* Fishbowl Activity * Four Corners Debate * Jigsaw Activity * Socratic Seminar * Stations Activity (Rotations of Documents, Tasks) * Structured Academic Controversy * Taking a Stand on Controversial Issues (Student Spectrum) * Think, Pair, Share

FIGURE 4.5 Common Social Studies Instructional Strategies

To support a thematic course in which you will rely less upon a cover-to-cover textbook reading, the use of primary and secondary sources becomes paramount. As most history teachers know, it is important to have students engage with evidence—both primary and secondary—to grasp a fuller meaning of historical attitudes, processes, and developments. When using such evidence, it is crucial to provide the necessary historical context and have students tap into their own prior knowledge or interest in the topic. Once students have that necessary context, then they can dive into their analysis of the sources. As author and educational professor Keith C. Barton notes, primary and secondary sources "can create personal connections to history," and visual evidence, such as photographs, advertisements, and art, can help students access information they might not otherwise glean from written sources (Barton 2005, 751). As teachers, we need to find ways to use evidence to spark students' questions and lines of inquiry, and we need to give students opportunities to evaluate the thoughts and perspectives of various actors in a historical event.

THEMATIC TEACHING IN ACTION: Elements of the Thematic Lesson

For the lesson on Chinese exclusion and Chinese resistance, we carefully considered the types of sources we wanted our students to examine. We first provide students with the historical context of late-nineteenth-century society, a period of intensive industrial growth and competition among immigrant and native-born workers for new wage labor jobs. When teaching thematically, it is important to provide the necessary historical context surrounding the primary source documents so all students have the same knowledge base. Since you are not following a standard chronological approach, historical context becomes essential; students may not have the background information to engage fully with documents on their own. Textbooks can often provide this common knowledge base, and we often assign students passages from the textbook so we can front-load course content. Then we examine primary and scholarly sources to explore greater nuance, deeper meaning, and multiple perspectives during class time as students are ready to evaluate the legal restrictions on Chinese immigrants from excerpts of the 1882 Chinese Exclusion Act. Having them develop questions like who was affected by this law and who was technically excluded could be a good starting point of discussion. Since part of our goal is for students to understand why such legal restrictions barred most Chinese from legally entering the country, they might read passages from anti-Chinese groups like the Workingman's Party in California or look at political cartoons from the national group the Knights of Labor's perspective. The Chinese and their allies in the United States as well as those in China did not simply accept these new restrictions without protest. Since not all supported this contentious law, students should also investigate legal challenges to the Chinese Exclusion Act, such as *Wong Kim Ark v. United States*. In 1898, the Supreme Court ruled that Wong Kim Ark, who was born in California, was a U.S. citizen by birth, so the Chinese Exclusion Act did not apply to him and other Chinese Americans born in the United States. By analyzing petitions by Chinese American merchants or by learning about the 1905 Chinese boycott of U.S. goods, students can appreciate the numerous ways the Chinese people applied political and economic pressure on the U.S. government. These various sources can give students some insight into why the Chinese Exclusion Act was passed and how it affected those who experienced it. Again, the strategic use of primary and secondary sources in a thematic course can help free you from the chronology of the textbook and allow you to highlight diverse perspectives in history.

As busy teachers, we often rely on vetted, professional resources to help us find tested instructional strategies as well as engaging primary and secondary source documents. Here are some of our favorites. In addition to providing strategies and sources, these resources have helped us provide more inclusive content and teach history through multiple perspectives.

The final part of this section of the lesson plan template is an *inclusion and engagement element.* As you considered your personal motivation for developing a thematic course in Chapter 1, you may have considered this as an opportunity to include more diverse voices throughout history and to engage students in a way that may be difficult in a chronological course. Those are certainly two key reasons we moved to a thematic approach. This part of the template gives you space to explicitly identify how you will build an inclusive lesson that engages your students. Although you may have had students read soldiers' diaries from the American Civil War in the past, now you want your lesson to include letters women wrote to their husbands who were at war and the impact those letters had on desertion in the military. This is where you consider present-day events or issues in the world or country today that connect to the historical lesson you are planning to teach. Consider starting your lesson with an examination of that event so students feel connected to the material before you even get to the history. Alternatively, you may tap into students' prior knowledge, engaging them by bridging the gap between what they already know and what they will learn in the lesson. Although elements of inclusion and engagement may have come up naturally in your lessons, we dedicated space on the template so teachers can be very intentional about including these elements, as they are key to student learning.

Assessments and Accommodations

The concluding section of our lesson plan template gives you space to plan how you will assess students and how you might modify your lesson for diverse learners (see Figure 4.6).

Assessment: How do you know that students have achieved the learning objective?	
Modifications/Accommodations: How can you provide the necessary modifications or accommodations for special education/English language learner students to achieve the learning objective?	

FIGURE 4.6 Lesson Template: Assessments and Accommodations

Our goal as teachers is not only to *teach* the material to students but to ensure they have *learned* it. It is important to assess student learning by the end of each lesson to make sure we have met our learning objective and students can successfully answer the learning focus question. This process puts the student in the role of budding historian, effectively analyzing historical content and evaluating its significance. Just as the instructional strategies you use will vary, so should your assessments. Checking for student understanding can be a quick verbal check with each student in the five minutes before the end of the period or a short written assignment where students answer the lesson focus question, or the assessment can be built into the lesson itself, checking for student understanding as you go. Our examples in Chapters 5 and 6 will demonstrate two ways we assess student learning at the end of a class period.

Finally, it is important that teachers plan how they might modify each lesson and assessment for diverse learners. This is equally true in a thematic course as it is in a chronological one. But a thematic course might incorporate more primary source documents that include arcane or unfamiliar language that can be challenging for students to read. Consider providing students with a summary of the document before they read it. Creating strategic partnerships, such as pairing English language learners with native English speakers, might also help facilitate student understanding of the material. Other modifications might be to shorten difficult documents, to preview challenging vocabulary words, or to provide sentence starters when assigning written work. Some students may need more time to process the information, so offering extensions can be a helpful support. These simple accommodations and modifications can be essential to providing access and opportunities for all students to learn.

A Preview of Thematic Teaching in Action: Creating Thematic Lesson Plans

Now that we have gone through the components of our lesson plan template, Chapters 5 and 6 will illustrate how we utilized that template with two of our lesson plans. These two lesson plans use a different approach to thematic lesson planning, one spanning a broad expanse of time and one covering a narrower period. A thematic approach to teaching history easily allows for single lessons to cover decades or even centuries, giving students an opportunity to examine continuity and change over time or long-term cause-and-effect patterns for a given topic. Some topics in which we cover a broad period of time in a single lesson include push and pull factors for immigration, Black Americans' access to education over time, the course and consequences of U.S. imperialism in the Philippines, and the LGBTQIA+ rights movement from the late 1960s to the present day. For these topics, it makes sense to cover a longer expanse of time in a single one- or two-day lesson so students can follow a particular thread through time. This approach allows students to effectively make connections between the past and the present.

Other lesson plan topics, however, may be better centered on a narrow period. This approach might work best for a lesson on Japanese incarceration, for example. Rather than tracing the history of Japanese Americans over a broad period, teaching a single lesson focusing on the incarceration of the Japanese allows students to situate the event in the broader context of World War II and dive deep into that one topic. Additional topics in which a narrower focus would be appropriate include women's roles in the American Revolution, the visibility of LGBTQIA+ artists during the Harlem Renaissance, and support and opposition of the Vietnam War. These lessons are more like those found in a traditional, chronological course, which is great! If you have been teaching for years and have lesson plans you love, you can use them in your thematic course. They would just be situated in a thematic unit that supports your course theme rather than a traditional unit that centers on a particular period.

Throughout the book, we have been highlighting examples of "Thematic Teaching in Action," providing you with models of how we designed and implemented our thematic course to serve as a guide as you develop your own course. As teachers, we know those daily lessons are crucial to creating a class that is engaging, is conducive to learning, and adheres to required state and district standards. So we are dedicating two chapters to "Thematic Teaching in Action: Lesson Planning," diving deep into all the elements covered in this chapter. In Chapter 5, we demonstrate a lesson centered on a concept that spans a broad period, the evolution of voting rights for Black Americans. In Chapter 6, the lesson focuses on a much narrower time, the efforts of women during World War II. For both examples, we walk you through the lesson plans and handouts that accompany the lessons. With each lesson, you will see how we incorporated an inquiry-based approach, along with elements of a thematic lesson, and how we assessed student learning. We hope these examples provide you with a clear idea of what day-to-day lessons can look like in a thematic course.

Chapter in Review

Let's take a moment to review. In this chapter, we:

- Discussed the various elements that go into a thematic lesson plan, including:
  - Use of inquiry-based questions
  - Focus on student engagement and inclusion
  - Ways to assess for understanding

- Introduced two types of lesson plans that we will delve into more depth:
  - One that spans a broad time period (Chapter 5)
  - One that spans a narrow time period (Chapter 6)

5

THEMATIC TEACHING IN ACTION
Broad Time Period Lesson on Voting Rights

DEVELOPING DAILY LESSON PLANS is often a fulfilling and creative experience for teachers. Although it is important that teachers develop the structure of a course and the flow of a thematic unit, it is the day-to-day lessons where we can put that big-picture planning into action to interact with students, which is why we teach. In the previous chapter, we introduced our lesson planning template and discussed the ingredients necessary to create a daily lesson plan. We also provided a brief rationale for developing either a broad or narrow period lesson plan.

Throughout the book, we have been providing examples of thematic teaching in action, sharing how we created our own thematic course, including the development of our course and unit themes, as well as mapping out the flow of our units. The lesson plan process is such a crucial ingredient to student learning, so we provide two entire chapters demonstrating this thematic teaching in action. As this type of lesson plan might be novel to even the most veteran teachers, we hope you find our example a helpful guide to this type of approach!

Building a Lesson That Spans a Broad Period of Time

When deciding which lessons should cover a broad period, consider ones in which key developments change or similar patterns emerge across time. The history of citizenship and suffrage rights can provide one example of such a development. In a traditional, chronological history course, it is difficult for students to understand how voting rights for Black Americans evolved over time. This makes it an ideal topic to develop into a broad period lesson rather than a one-day focus on events occurring in the early 1960s. The lesson we provide here is from our thematic unit on the African American Freedom Rights Movement. Before we get into the lesson itself, look at our unit map to see where this lesson plan fits into our broader unit (see Figure 5.1).

THEMATIC UNIT: African American Freedom Rights Movement

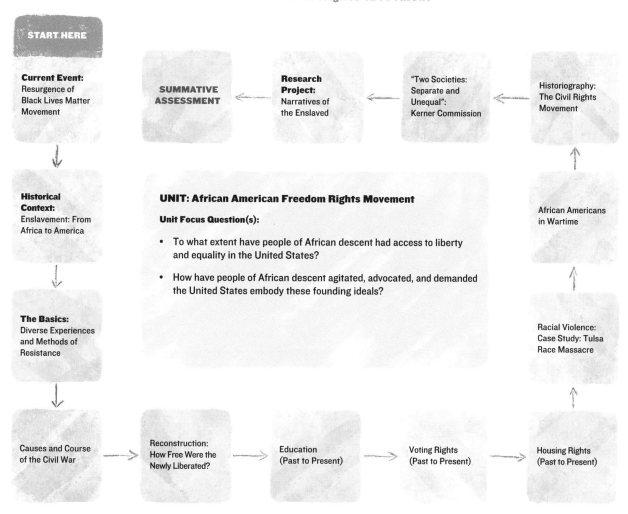

START HERE

Current Event: Resurgence of Black Lives Matter Movement

SUMMATIVE ASSESSMENT

Research Project: Narratives of the Enslaved

"Two Societies: Separate and Unequal": Kerner Commission

Historiography: The Civil Rights Movement

Historical Context: Enslavement: From Africa to America

African Americans in Wartime

UNIT: African American Freedom Rights Movement

Unit Focus Question(s):

- To what extent have people of African descent had access to liberty and equality in the United States?

- How have people of African descent agitated, advocated, and demanded the United States embody these founding ideals?

The Basics: Diverse Experiences and Methods of Resistance

Racial Violence: Case Study: Tulsa Race Massacre

Causes and Course of the Civil War

Reconstruction: How Free Were the Newly Liberated?

Education (Past to Present)

Voting Rights (Past to Present)

Housing Rights (Past to Present)

FIGURE 5.1 Thematic Unit Map: "African American Freedom Rights Movement"

You can see that we start in the present day, as we do with all our units. Then the unit progresses in chronological order from the African slave trade through the Civil War and Reconstruction, then moves through the twentieth century and back to the modern era. For three of our lesson topics, education, voting rights (highlighted in Figure 5.1), and housing rights, it made sense to create lessons that spanned a broad period, as each of these developments changed dramatically for Black Americans from the Civil War to the present day.

Though less conventional, the broad thematic lesson may be a better method for some historical content than the traditional, narrow period lesson. Some aspects of history demonstrate long-term patterns of development, especially when examining various protest movements. Movements that occur over extended periods of time, such as the push for voting rights, can be ideal material for a broad thematic lesson, and they can help students analyze patterns of comparison, causation, and continuity and change over time more effectively. For instance, a traditional lesson on the 1965 Voting Rights Act can demonstrate why this legislation was enacted and the impact it made in a brief period, but the broader approach can show the difficulties of more than a century's worth of agitating, advocating, and demanding changes to the franchise. It is important for students to understand that major changes do not simply happen overnight; it can take decades, even centuries to realize change. Furthermore, the narrow approach to the Voting Rights Act runs the risk of centering top-down administrative decision-making, whereas the broad approach can highlight the efforts of various grassroots agents across a longer spectrum of time. The traditional lesson may also mislead students to believe the 1965 legislation was a permanent solution to voting access in the country; however, a broad thematic lesson can illuminate a process that continues to expand and contract throughout the nation today, making this historical development more relevant to students' lives.

Developing and teaching one lesson that spans such a long time might be new for even the most veteran teachers. So we will use our lesson on voting rights to illustrate how you can create a thematic lesson that traces one topic over multiple decades. In the next part of this chapter, we break down each section of our lesson plan, highlight aspects of the document students interact with through the lesson, and provide samples of student work. In our broad thematic lesson on Black American voting rights, we incorporated our essential ingredients of inquiry-based learning, engaging students with topical subject matter, and centering the perspectives of marginalized groups, specifically Black Americans. The lesson plan asks students to evaluate the relative limitations and gains of voting rights between the Reconstruction Era and today, to consider current efforts to change voting laws, and to analyze the long-term efforts of Black Americans and their allies to expand access to the franchise.

NAVIGATING PROVOCATIVE CONTENT: TEACHING FOR UNDERSTANDING

With this voting rights lesson and others that involve potentially provocative content, it is critical to make sure that your focus is on student understanding of a nuanced and complex history. You may face certain reactions when teaching thematically including community presumptions of your agenda as the teacher and notions that students must leave "feeling" a certain way—delighted, guilty, or disgusted—about history. In response to some of these potential community reactions, we have used scholarly writing on the perils of when the desire to feel a certain way about a nation's history overtakes the simple need to understand it. One great resource we use with our students and with parents is Daniel Immerwahr's "History Isn't Just for Patriots: We Teach Students How to Understand the U.S., Not to Love It—or Hate It" (2020). As Immerwahr relates, history teachers create "curriculums around what students will learn rather than how they'll feel." Being direct and upfront with your students and your parent community about your goal of teaching history for understanding, not to instill patriotism or shame, may help alleviate some concerns that you have a particular agenda you are trying to push.

Unlike many other academic subjects, there is an expectation that students will emerge from history classes with a keen sense of patriotism and national pride. Textbooks can reinforce this notion by presenting a dominant narrative that carefully selects events to shine a positive light on accomplishments and omitting any blemishes that do not support this perspective. By supplementing textbook accounts with primary and secondary sources, we can provide diverse perspectives and teach students the skills to be critical thinkers and readers. That way, they can *understand* what has happened in the past, which is more important than simply feeling one way or the other about it! ●

An Overview of the Black American Voting Rights Lesson

For this section, we have included a sample lesson plan using our template from Chapter 4 and our document for students (see Figures 5.2 and 5.3). As we dissect the different sections of this lesson plan, we will incorporate elements from the student document and examples of student work. Since this type of lesson plan spans a broad period of time, it is important to consider the order in which we present the material to our students. We begin in the present day to engage students' curiosity by connecting the historical content to recent developments with passage of contemporary voting laws. Students may naturally question how we got to this point today with our voting laws. We want to provide the necessary historical context and content so students can answer this question for themselves. For students to make these past-to-present connections, we must go back to the inception of federal voting rights for Black Americans starting with the Fifteenth Amendment to the Constitution. This creates a starting point for a timeline that spans 150 years of history. Then we trace the key milestones in Black American voting from there, so students can understand the causal relations among these events, as they determine how and why access to the franchise has changed and remained the same.

In this lesson, after we engage students with current events, we tap into their prior knowledge about political rights and limitations during the Reconstruction Era through the mid-twentieth century. Using a combination of primary source documents and videos, students work in pairs and independently to investigate relative voter access and the impact it has had on marginalized groups. We present this broad history chronologically so students will be less likely to get "lost" in over 150 years of events concerning voting rights for Black Americans. Finally, we conclude the lesson with a formative assessment that requires students to address the lesson focus question on voting rights accessibility across that broad period of time.

LESSON PLAN: Voting Rights

Lesson Title: Voting Rights for Black Americans	**Time Required:** 90-minute block

Unit Title: African American Freedom Rights Movement

Content Standard(s):	**11.10 Students analyze the development of federal civil rights and voting rights.** 6. Analyze the passage and effects of civil rights and voting rights legislation (e.g., 1964 Civil Rights Act, Voting Rights Act of 1965) and the Twenty-Fourth Amendment, with an emphasis on equality of access to education and to the political process.
Course Big-Picture Question:	✳ How have historically marginalized groups agitated, advocated, and demanded the United States embody its founding ideals of liberty and equality? ✳ Evaluate the extent to which various groups were successful in attaining their rights to liberty and equality.
Unit-Level Focus Questions:	✳ To what extent have people of African descent had access to liberty and equality in the United States? ✳ How have people of African descent agitated, advocated, and demanded the United States embody these founding ideals?
Lesson Focus Question:	Evaluate the extent that Black Americans attained greater access to voting rights, weighing limitations and gains between the Reconstruction Era and today.
Learning Objective:	Students will be able to address the learning focus question using both historical content and the historical thinking skill of continuity and change over time.

Historical Content	Instructional Strategy and Sources
✳ The Fifteenth Amendment ✳ Jim Crow barriers to voting (poll taxes, grandfather clauses, literacy tests, violence, etc.) ✳ Selma marches to Montgomery ✳ Voting Rights Act of 1965 ✳ *Shelby County v. Holder and* recent voting legislation	✳ Tapping into prior knowledge ✳ Primary source analysis (video "Selma 50 Years Later: Remembering Bloody Sunday"; text excerpts from the 1965 Voting Rights Act) ✳ Simulation of literacy test (Louisiana Literacy Test) ✳ Examination of present-day voting legislation (Brennan Center article)
Historical Thinking	**Inclusion and Engagement**
Continuity and change over time Primary source analysis (text and video)	Current event connection with examination of present-day voting laws; agency of the Black community

Assessment: How do you know that students have achieved the learning objective?	Students will complete an exit ticket at the end of the lesson responding to the lesson focus question. Strong responses will cite specific historical evidence and weigh both limitations and gains from Reconstruction to the present day.
Modifications/Accommodations: How can you provide the necessary modifications or accommodations for special education/English language learner students to achieve the learning objective?	All of the following will be provided as needed: ✳ Primary sources can be further excerpted ✳ Vocabulary ✳ Extended time ✳ Sentence starters ✳ Option for verbal response as opposed to written ✳ Access to notes

FIGURE 5.2 Sample Lesson Plan for Teachers: Broad Time Period

VOTING RIGHTS FOR BLACK AMERICANS (PAST TO PRESENT)

CONNECTING WITH THE PAST

✳ Skim through the Brennan Center for Justice article "Voting Laws Roundup: October 2021" on their website. Take note of some of the new restrictive laws and some of the new expanded laws passed by various states.

New Restrictive Laws	New Expansive Laws

Lesson Focus Question: *Evaluate the extent that Black Americans attained greater access to voting rights, weighing limitations and gains between the Reconstruction Era and today.*

RECONSTRUCTION AND JIM CROW

1. Reflecting back on our unit thus far, what do you know about Black American voting rights (and obstacles to voting) in U.S. history?

SIMULATION: LITERACY TEST

2. As an individual, take ten minutes to attempt to complete the entire Louisiana literacy test (thirty tasks).[1] What do you notice? What are your thoughts on the test? After ten minutes, we will discuss your findings as a class.

SELMA

3. In 1965, Civil Rights activists marched from Selma, Alabama, to the capital city of Montgomery, demonstrating their desire to exercise their constitutional right to vote. Among the activists were John Lewis, Dr. Martin Luther King Jr., Amelia Boynton Robinson, and Diane Nash. Watch the documentary "Selma 50 Years Later: Remembering Bloody Sunday" on YouTube™. Take notes in the space below and prepare to share your findings with the class.

---

1   The Louisiana Literacy Test can be found online as a pdf (Ferris State University). It consists of thirty questions.

FIGURE 5.3 Sample Lesson Plan for Students: Broad Time Period *(continues)*

VOTING RIGHTS ACT OF 1965

4. After the marches in Selma, President Lyndon B. Johnson signed the Voting Rights Act of 1965 into law. Read and prepare to share your findings on the excerpt of the act below. What does the Voting Rights Act of 1965 do? What previous policies did this law attempt to address? How do you know?

Source: The Voting Rights Act of 1965

"SEC. 2. No voting qualification or prerequisite to voting, or standard, practice, or procedure shall be imposed or applied by any State or political subdivision to deny or abridge the right of any citizen of the United States to vote on account of race or color. . . .

"SEC. 3(b) If in a proceeding instituted by the Attorney General under any statute to enforce the guarantees of the fifteenth amendment in any State or political subdivision the court finds that a test or device has been used for the purpose or with the effect of denying or abridging the right of any citizen of the United States to vote on account of race or color, it shall suspend the use of tests and devices in such State or political subdivisions as the court shall determine is appropriate and for such period as it deems necessary."

5. In 2013, the Supreme Court modified the Voting Rights Act of 1965 in the *Shelby County v. Holder* case. This made it easier for states to pass new voting laws. Some argue that these new laws create challenges for historically marginalized groups to exercise their rights to vote, but others say they are intended to protect voter legitimacy.

   Working with a partner and using the Brennan Center article, use an example of a restrictive or expansive voting bill or law that has been proposed or passed. Complete the chart below:

With your partner:	
What does the bill or law state?	
Which state proposed or passed the legislation?	
How might this bill or law impact Black Americans or other historically marginalized groups?	
Whole-class share-out:	
Take notes on the various bills your classmates found.	

EXIT TICKET

Formative Assessment: Evaluate the extent that Black Americans attained greater access to voting rights, weighing limitations and gains between the Reconstruction Era and today.

FIGURE 5.3 *(continued)* Sample Lesson Plan for Students: Broad Time Period

An Inquiry-Based Approach: Voting Rights

For the first section of the lesson plan, we used state standards and our course big-picture and unit-level focus questions to determine our lesson focus question and learning objective. In the California Framework, federal civil and voting rights are the focus of one of our content standards (see Figure 5.4). Although it references the "development" of these rights, the examples provided in the standard focus on top-down federal legislation from the mid-1960s. While these acts and the amendment are important, we want our students to understand the denial of voting rights and the protest movements that led to the passage of this legislation. This is an opportunity to center the voices of Black American activists and their allies who have been fighting for decades to secure voting rights for this community. As you evaluate which content standard your lesson will address, be sure to consider whose voices might be missing. Students should see how and why this legislation was passed, who was responsible, and its impact over the short term and long term.

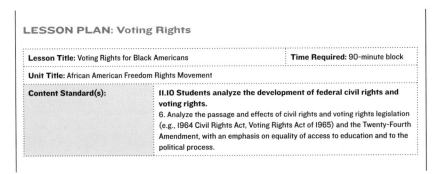

LESSON PLAN: Voting Rights

Lesson Title: Voting Rights for Black Americans	Time Required: 90-minute block
Unit Title: African American Freedom Rights Movement	

Content Standard(s):	**11.10 Students analyze the development of federal civil rights and voting rights.** 6. Analyze the passage and effects of civil rights and voting rights legislation (e.g., 1964 Civil Rights Act, Voting Rights Act of 1965) and the Twenty-Fourth Amendment, with an emphasis on equality of access to education and to the political process.

FIGURE 5.4 Sample Lesson Plan for Teachers: Content Standards

To address our big-picture question for this thematic unit on the African American Freedom Rights Movement, our unit-level focus questions center the perspectives and agency of people of African descent in obtaining liberty and equality (see Figure 5.5). The lesson on voting rights explores a broad period, so we want a lesson focus question/prompt that makes this historical development relevant but also unresolved for our students. History can be considered "boring" to students if they think it is merely something that occurred in the past and has been settled already. Getting them to see how these events continue to affect them and evolve over time not only gains their attention but prepares them to actively participate in the nation's decision-making process.

Course Big-Picture Question:	✳ How have historically marginalized groups agitated, advocated, and demanded the United States embody its founding ideals of liberty and equality? ✳ Evaluate the extent to which various groups were successful in attaining their rights to liberty and equality.
Unit-Level Focus Questions:	✳ To what extent have people of African descent had access to liberty and equality in the United States? ✳ How have people of African descent agitated, advocated, and demanded the United States embody these founding ideals?
Lesson Focus Question:	Evaluate the extent that Black Americans attained greater access to voting rights, weighing limitations and gains between the Reconstruction Era and today.
Learning Objective:	Students will be able to address the learning focus question using both historical content and the historical thinking skill of continuity and change over time.

FIGURE 5.5 Sample Lesson Plan for Teachers: Inquiry-Based Approach

Again, we want to avoid telling the class *what to think*; our objective with this open-ended lesson focus question/prompt is to have students practice *how to think* by using an array of evidence to support their claims. This becomes even more important as debates over Critical Race Theory make history instruction more controversial than ever. Developing lesson topics from district or statewide standards can provide a clear rationale for teacher decision-making in response to potential administrative or community pushback. Also, having students analyze document evidence for themselves and arrive at conclusions based on the facts is not simply good pedagogical practice but crucial for the health of a responsible citizenry.

Our learning objective is for students to address our lesson focus question/prompt and practice the historical thinking skill of continuity and change over time. This skill would be hard to use if students only examined events from the mid-1960s! It is necessary, therefore, to explore deeper into the context of events from the late nineteenth and early twentieth centuries and extend that knowledge through to today to understand the pattern of how things may have changed—for better or worse—and how they may seem to remain the same. Analyzing continuity and change over time patterns requires students to engage in chronologically ordered thinking and to compare periods of time before and after a key turning point event. We use the 1965 Voting Rights Act as that turning point event, asking students to consider what led up to its passage and the impact it had on Black Americans. Furthermore, students will investigate legislation made in the aftermath of *Shelby County v. Holder* (2013) that limits and expands voter access, as well as the continuing impact of this Supreme Court decision, which itself might be considered a turning point.

Elements of the Thematic Lesson: Voting Rights

This next section focuses on the crucial elements of any lesson plan: the historical content, thinking skills, instructional strategies and resources used, and considerations for inclusion and student engagement. Also, this is a good place to ensure that these crucial elements in the lesson plan connect with our essential ingredients of inquiry-based learning, engaging students with topical subject matter, and centering the perspectives of marginalized groups.

For the "Historical Content" section of the lesson plan template, we brainstormed a list of what we wanted students to know or remember, especially as context for the Voting Rights Act of 1965 (see Figure 5.6). The amount of information we might list could easily get overwhelming, so we tried to home in on the most essential information. Another consideration we had in making this list was the selection of relevant and unsettled content to engage students' attention more effectively. We decided that students should know the Reconstruction Era amendments, especially the Fifteenth, which states the right to vote cannot be refused to people due to their race, color, or former status of enslavement by either the states or the federal government. The Jim Crow laws passed in Southern states beginning in the late nineteenth century would also be essential information; these acts aimed to maintain a racially segregated society, and they constructed significant barriers to voting through poll taxes and literacy tests, enforced with terror and violence. The 1965 Selma marches to Montgomery provide immediate context for growing national support of the Voting Rights Act. Grassroots efforts to end voter suppression in Alabama led to deadly confrontations between peaceful protesters and state-backed mob violence. Finally, the Supreme Court case *Shelby County v. Holder* serves as our way to show students the continuing relevance of the Voting Rights Act and how current-day legislation expands and limits people's access to voting rights.

When crafting our lesson focus question, we had already determined that continuity and change over time would be our skills focus for this lesson (see Figure 5.7). The "continuity and change over time" prompt is appropriate for the topic since we are asking students to trace the gains and setbacks of voting rights over 150 years. Since students will be investigating several primary sources, we will use guiding questions and provide think-pair-share opportunities to help students understand the excerpts of long documents and filmed interviews to help them prepare to use this evidence.

As part of our focus on inclusion and engagement, we begin by having students read an article by the Brennan Center for Justice (2021),

Historical Content

* The Fifteenth Amendment
* Jim Crow barriers to voting (poll taxes, grandfather clauses, literacy tests, violence, etc.)
* Selma marches to Montgomery
* Voting Rights Act of 1965
* *Shelby County v. Holder and recent* voting legislation

FIGURE 5.6 Historical Content: Lesson on Voting Rights

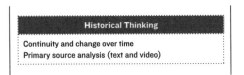

Historical Thinking

Continuity and change over time
Primary source analysis (text and video)

FIGURE 5.7 Historical Thinking Skills: Lesson on Voting Rights

a nonprofit law and policy advocacy group (see Figure 5.8). The article provides a recap of new 2021 voter registration laws and proposed acts that expand voter access and/or limit it.

This legislation, the Brennan Center for Justice argues, was spurred in response to unprecedented voter turnout in the 2020 election and the COVID-19 pandemic. This lesson "hook" has students skim through some of this legislation that affects voter access today (see Figure 5.9). As soon-to-be voters, students should be aware of how mutable access to voting can be. Once students feel a personal connection to the lesson topic, they are more eager to dive into the history behind it.

FIGURE 5.8 Inclusion and Engagement: Lesson on Voting Rights

VOTING RIGHTS FOR BLACK AMERICANS (PAST TO PRESENT)

CONNECTING WITH THE PAST

* Skim through the Brennan Center for Justice article "Voting Laws Roundup: October 2021" on their website. Take note of some of the new restrictive laws and some of the new expanded laws passed by various states.

New Restrictive Laws	New Expansive Laws

FIGURE 5.9 Sample Lesson Prompt for Students: Connecting with the Past

After piquing students' interest in the present day, we then tap into students' prior knowledge about voting rights and ways access was limited for Black Americans. Early in the lesson, we ask students what they already know about Black American voting rights throughout U.S. history (see Figure 5.10).

RECONSTRUCTION AND JIM CROW

I. Reflecting back on our unit thus far, what do you know about Black American voting rights (and obstacles to voting) in U.S. history?

FIGURE 5.10 Sample Lesson Prompt for Students: Reconstruction and Jim Crow

When we taught this lesson, we found that many students knew about the Fifteenth Amendment, and some referenced the Nineteenth Amendment (women's suffrage) as well. Although a few shared prior knowledge about poll taxes and literacy tests, several students added the use of violence to bar Black American voters from the polls, particularly the role of groups like the Ku Klux Klan. Since this lesson will cover such a broad period, we want to ensure all students have this baseline knowledge before moving forward (see Figure 5.11).

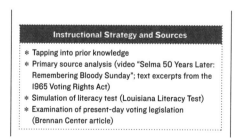

FIGURE 5.11 Instructional Strategy and Sources: Lesson on Voting Rights

One strategy we routinely use that helps students acquire this baseline knowledge and feel confident sharing findings in a whole-class discussion is think-pair-share. Rather than cold-calling students, we provide the question in advance and in writing to the entire class; they are given time to think and write down their ideas; and then they discuss what they wrote with a partner before being asked to share information with the whole class. All are instructed to record their partners' and classmates' responses in addition to their own. Though it can lengthen the time of discussion, it helps build a supportive classroom community and more effectively engages students in the lesson. After students have had the opportunity to share what they know, we fill in the gaps by providing any missing historical information and correcting any misconceptions about the content.

After ensuring all students know about Black Americans' enfranchisement after the Civil War, as well as the obstacles and barriers that prevented the exercise of these rights in Reconstruction's aftermath, we want students to uncover some key milestones of voting in the twentieth century. An important way to acquire this essential information is by having students analyze primary and secondary sources to draw their own conclusions.

For this next step, we gave the class ten minutes to complete a literacy test used by the state of Louisiana to provide students an experiential lens into disenfranchisement (see Figures 5.12 and 5.13). This thirty-question test, recreated from memory by those who took it, provides brainteaser obstacles to determine whether the potential voter could read and write. We have students think-pair-share their reactions after completing this test, discussing especially why this could be one effective way to bar someone from the franchise. Students often questioned whether there should be voter qualifications, such as literacy, voter identification, a lack of a criminal record, and so on, and who those restrictions might impact.

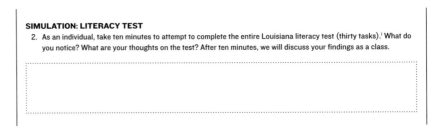

SIMULATION: LITERACY TEST

2. As an individual, take ten minutes to attempt to complete the entire Louisiana literacy test (thirty tasks).[1] What do you notice? What are your thoughts on the test? After ten minutes, we will discuss your findings as a class.

FIGURE 5.12 Sample Lesson Prompt for Students: Simulation of a Literacy Test

The State of Louisiana

Literacy Test (This test is to be given to anyone who cannot prove a fifth grade education.)

Do what you are told to do in each statement, nothing more, nothing less. Be careful as one wrong answer denotes failure of the test. You have 10 minutes to complete the test.

1. Draw a line around the number or letter of this sentence.

2. Draw a line under the last word of this line.

3. Cross out the longest word in this line.

4. Draw a line around the shortest word in this line.

5. Circle the first, first letter of the alphabet in this line.

6. In the space below draw three circles, one inside (engulfed by) the other.

FIGURE 5.13 Instructions and Initial Questions from the "Louisiana Literacy Test," c. 1964

Once students examine some of the barriers Black Americans faced when attempting to exercise their right to vote, we have them listen to firsthand accounts to appreciate the perspective of grassroots activists. Students watch the testimony of participants and video news footage of the initial Selma March to Montgomery, called Bloody Sunday (*Los Angeles Times* 2015). On that day, law enforcement aided by a white mob attacked nonviolent protesters on the Edmund Pettus Bridge in Selma, Alabama.

After watching the documentary, students share their reactions and findings with the class. Some may discuss thoughts on police violence (see Figure 5.14). Others may argue that nonviolent protest and the use of moral suasion, though challenging, were most effective in creating national public sympathy for the marchers, especially with a media presence on the scene.

"In the [video] scene, police officers were quick to act and they didn't actually give the activists any time to run away. They actually threatened the marchers, who were protesting peacefully, and immediately resorted to using brutal force. They showed no sympathy to the African American marchers and treated them like criminals—it was hard to watch."

Erin | student

SELMA

3. In 1965, Civil Rights activists marched from Selma, Alabama, to the capital city of Montgomery, demonstrating their desire to exercise their constitutional right to vote. Among the activists were John Lewis, Dr. Martin Luther King Jr., Amelia Boynton Robinson, and Diane Nash. Watch the documentary "Selma 50 Years Later: Remembering Bloody Sunday" on YouTube™. Take notes in the space below and prepare to share your findings with the class.

FIGURE 5.14 Sample Lesson Prompt for Students: "Selma 50 Years Later" Video Analysis

After discussing the video, students read and analyze excerpts from the Voting Rights Act of 1965 (National Archives), explaining what it proposed to do and why it was necessary (see Figure 5.15).

VOTING RIGHTS ACT OF 1965

4. After the marches in Selma, President Lyndon B. Johnson signed the Voting Rights Act of 1965 into law. Read and prepare to share your findings on the excerpt of the act below. What does the Voting Rights Act of 1965 do? What previous policies did this law attempt to address? How do you know?

> **Source:** The Voting Rights Act of 1965
>
> "SEC. 2. No voting qualification or prerequisite to voting, or standard, practice, or procedure shall be imposed or applied by any State or political subdivision to deny or abridge the right of any citizen of the United States to vote on account of race or color. . . .
>
> "SEC. 3(b) If in a proceeding instituted by the Attorney General under any statute to enforce the guarantees of the fifteenth amendment in any State or political subdivision the court finds that a test or device has been used for the purpose or with the effect of denying or abridging the right of any citizen of the United States to vote on account of race or color, it shall suspend the use of tests and devices in such State or political subdivisions as the court shall determine is appropriate and for such period as it deems necessary."

FIGURE 5.15 Sample Lesson Prompt for Students: Analysis of the Voting Rights Act of 1965

By presenting the Voting Rights Act after students watch the perspectives of Selma marchers, it challenges the narrative that Congress and President Lyndon B. Johnson were the impetus behind this legislation. Rather, students can see its passage was a result of pressures from various activist groups like the Selma marchers and those that came before them. The groundwork had been laid long before the act was passed in 1965. In a chronological course, the top-down explanation for the Voting Rights Act's passage is emphasized. However, in a thematic course, teachers have the flexibility to teach a broader period in a single lesson, so students can fully appreciate the evolution of historical developments, like voting rights.

> "In response to the protests, three [Selma] marches, the Voting Rights Act was passed. They [Voting Rights Act of 1965] make it so the courts and justice department can determine if it's obstructing people's rights. If it was obstructing the right to vote, then federal officials would go in. If voter turnout was low, the federal government would be alerted. It would trigger the courts or justice department to look into if the state was restricting people's right to vote."
>
> **Jacqueline** | student

In the example at left, a student made connections between the documentary and the excerpt from the Voting Rights Act. She explained that the 1965 law addressed the disenfranchisement of Black Americans, especially in Southern states. As Jacqueline pointed out, the Voting Rights Act provided a federal monitoring system to prevent voter restrictions on account of race and authorized government intervention if findings supported such obstruction was occurring. She identified the causal relationship between the Selma protests and the passage of the Voting Rights Act.

Not only do we try to emphasize the importance of the Voting Rights Act, what led to its passage, and how it provided greater access for Black Americans, we also want students to see the continuing importance of voting access and restrictions today. After providing brief context on *Shelby County v. Holder* (2013), a Supreme Court decision that made it easier for states to pass new voter laws, students skim the Brennan article that we used as a lesson "hook" once more. This time the task is for student teams to investigate one piece of legislation (their choice) and share their findings with the rest of the class more carefully (see Figure 5.16).

5. In 2013, the Supreme Court modified the Voting Rights Act of 1965 in the *Shelby County v. Holder* case. This made it easier for states to pass new voting laws. Some argue that these new laws create challenges for historically marginalized groups to exercise their rights to vote, but others say they are intended to protect voter legitimacy.

Working with a partner and using the Brennan Center article, use an example of a restrictive or expansive voting bill or law that has been proposed or passed. Complete the chart below:

With your partner:	
What does the bill or law state?	
Which state proposed or passed the legislation?	
How might this bill or law impact Black Americans or other historically marginalized groups?	
Whole-class share-out:	
Take notes on the various bills your classmates found.	

FIGURE 5.16 Sample Lesson Prompt for Students: Evaluating Restrictive and Expansive Voting Laws

At this point in the lesson, students have explored a wide range of events connected to Black Americans' relative access to voting rights between 1865 and the present day. Throughout the lesson, we attempt to engage students by showing the continuing relevance of voter legislation, highlighting Black American activism, and disrupting the notion that the 1965 Voting Rights Act settled the issue and is no longer important. Since this content spans over 150 years of history, the broad approach can help you and students effectively navigate the volume of information and more effectively see patterns of continuity and change over time.

Assessments and Accommodations: Voting Rights

After tapping into their prior knowledge regarding voting rights, examining primary and secondary sources from the 1960s through the present day, and investigating specific contemporary voter registration laws, students should be able to complete an exit ticket that responds to our lesson focus question. The exit ticket requires students to use specific historical evidence, pulled from the primary and secondary sources we examined in the lesson, and the historical thinking skill of continuity and change over time. Rather than checking for rote memorization, we expect students to demonstrate their content knowledge by crafting a clear argument that addresses the prompt and utilizing specific, accurate evidence to back up their claim. In general, however, we want to determine if students understand the content connected to our state standard, can demonstrate proficiency with crafting a historical argument, and are able to use factual details to support their assertions.

Since this is a lesson that spans more than a century, we are looking for students to make meaningful connections across that broad time. Again, one of the benefits of teaching history thematically is that events are not examined in isolation. In a chronological class, a lesson on the Voting Rights Act of 1965 is partnered with other lessons on the Civil Rights Movement, but that movement for rights is often situated in a larger unit during the Cold War era. In that case, students are not given the opportunity to fully understand the causes of the Civil Rights Movement nor its legacy. By providing a quick assessment at the end of this lesson, we can see if students understand the longer, more complex fight for voting rights (see Figure 5.17).

Assessment: How do you know that students have achieved the learning objective?	Students will complete an exit ticket at the end of the lesson responding to the lesson focus question. Strong responses will cite specific historical evidence and weigh both limitations and gains from Reconstruction to the present day.

FIGURE 5.17 Assessment: How do you know that students have achieved the learning objective?

SAMPLE LESSON PROMPT FOR STUDENTS: EXIT TICKET

EXIT TICKET:

Formative Assessment: Evaluate the extent that Black Americans attained greater access to voting rights, weighing limitations and gains between the Reconstruction Era and today.

"After the abolition of slavery, Jim Crow and voter suppression specifically targeted African American voters. Literacy tests and poll taxing all disproportionately affected Black voters . . . and threats and terrorism from white supremacists worked to withhold the ballot from them. After the Voting Rights Act was passed, African Americans were protected by law from being held back from the voting booth, specifically in six Southern states where voting rates of Black people were particularly low. However, in 2013, when sections 4 and 5 of the voting acts were repealed, those states, as well as all the others, could pass their own voting legislation, under the assumption that since voting rates have been equal for so long the U.S. doesn't have a problem with voting equity. Since then, new legislation has been passed that doesn't target minority voters, but it puts them at a disadvantage. Prohibiting early voting and closing polling places are just some examples of laws that create obstacles for people who are in the lower-income bracket (which still comprises minority racial groups) to cast their ballot."

Regan | student

In the preceding example, the student does an effective job connecting the broader idea about voting rights across the late nineteenth century through today. She referenced Jim Crow era restrictions and used the Voting Rights Act well in her response. Although the student does not discuss Black American activism and describes, but does not name, *Shelby County v. Holder*, her argument strongly supports a continuation of limits on Black Americans' voting access.

"Throughout American history, suffrage has been a key point of controversy and conflict. Despite the ratification of the Fifteenth Amendment in 1870, several Southern states strategically still passed restrictions to stop African Americans from voting in the form of literacy tests . . . grandfather clauses . . . and poll taxes. . . . However, eventually, beginning in the early twentieth century, African Americans began to gain liberty and equality in terms of voting rights. Firstly, in 1915, the Supreme Court deemed Grandfather Clauses to be unconstitutional. Next, in 1964, the Twenty-Fourth Amendment was ratified, which abolished poll taxes. In 1965, following the marches in Selma after which many African Americans marched from Selma, Alabama, to the capital city of Montgomery, President Lyndon B. Johnson signed the Voting Rights Act of 1965 into law. The Voting Rights Act named six Southern states and stated that they couldn't pass new voting laws without federal approval. Due to these laws, African Americans eventually gained access to liberty and equality in terms of voting rights, something which they should have received in 1870 itself with the ratification of the Fifteenth Amendment. In conclusion, despite not having liberty and equality in terms of . . . voting rights initially, eventually as the decades progressed, due to a combination of supreme court cases, and new laws being passed, African Americans have gained liberty and equality when pertaining to . . . voting rights."

Amitoj | student

In this second student example, we can clearly see the elements of our thematic lesson on display. The student brings in several pieces of historical content to make a persuasive argument that the Voting Rights Act was the result of a century-long struggle for Black Americans to achieve full voting rights. The student cites the Selma marches as contributing factors to the passage of the Voting Rights Act, understanding the power of grassroots activism. He has a solid grasp of how voting rights for Black Americans changed over time, demonstrating proficient use of the historical thinking skill we were addressing in this lesson. Had these topics been split into several different units throughout the course of a school year, as in a chronological course, this student would not be able to trace this evolution of voting rights in such a meaningful way. ●

The final consideration for our lesson is ways to modify the plan or provide accommodations for students with different learning needs or language barriers (see Figure 5.18). Our classrooms, like yours, are composed of individuals, and we want each student to meet the objectives and experience success.

Modifications/Accommodations: How can you provide the necessary modifications or accommodations for special education/English language learner students to achieve the learning objective?	All of the following will be provided as needed: * Primary sources can be further excerpted * Vocabulary * Extended time * Sentence starters * Option for verbal response as opposed to written * Access to notes

FIGURE 5.18 Modifications/Accommodations: How can you provide the necessary modifications or accommodations for special education/English language learner students to achieve the learning objective?

Considering the unique individuals in our classes, we wanted to keep in mind ways to make the content accessible even for students whose first language is not English or who may have difficulty with learning differences. The lesson requires a lot of different critical thinking, reading, and writing tasks, so we brainstormed some ways to address this by previewing difficult vocabulary in the Voting Rights Act or having students work together to paraphrase the content of the source to clarify its meaning. Many of our students require extended time on tasks, so being flexible about pacing or when assignments are due is an effective way to level the playing field. All students will have access to their notes for the exit ticket because our goal is not to measure rote memorization of facts discussed, but students' use of the information. Another modification would be to allow students to respond orally, rather than in writing. A few of our students needed additional scaffolds to help them understand the prompt and the structure of a paragraph. We offered a few simple sentence starters for this lesson:

❊ Between Reconstruction and today, Black Americans experienced improved access to voting rights. For example, . . .

❊ Between Reconstruction and today, Black Americans continue to have limited access to voting rights. For example, . . .

Both sentence starters elicit an either/or response: voting rights either changed by improving or remained the same by continuing to limit access. If your students are ready to expand their writing skills and engage in deeper analysis, have students contemplate the ways access to voting stayed the same *and* the ways in which it has changed over time. This last strategy for weighing the "gray" of the argument takes time and practice, as well as use of two-column charts and teacher modeling (see Figure 5.19).

Voting rights changed over time by . . .	Voting rights stayed the same by . . .
❊ The Voting Rights Act and the Twenty-Fourth Amendment bar the use of literacy tests and poll taxes. ❊ Some states passed recent legislation limiting access through voter identification requirements. ❊ Some states passed recent legislation expanding access to polls by allowing mail-in ballots.	❊ Some Southern states continue to limit voter access for historically marginalized groups. ❊ The methods have changed, but the impact has the same results by making voting more difficult.

FIGURE 5.19 Two-Column Chart on "Finding the Gray" of the Argument

We strive to differentiate instruction for our students who may have language or processing difficulties and also to provide students with expanded opportunities to advance their writing and thinking skills.

Putting It All Together: A Broad Time Period Lesson Plan

In this section highlighting a thematic lesson that spans a broad period, we walked through a lesson on voting rights using our lesson plan template, our student lesson document, and several student responses. We hope the step-by-step breakdown of our lesson demonstrates how you can create a lesson plan that spans multiple decades, as this might be a new concept for you. A good place to start is to review the thematic unit you developed while working through Chapter 3. Look at your unit map and select one lesson that may span a broad period or geographic place. Consider a big idea, issue, or conflict, perhaps one that spans several decades or even a century. As you develop this lesson idea, keep in mind our essential ingredients: inquiry-based learning, student engagement through relevant content, and inclusion of historically marginalized groups. Take the opportunity to engage your students' curiosity and understanding of history's continuing relevance. We have provided a blank template for you to develop this lesson plan (see Figure 5.20). You have got this!

Chapter in Review

Let's take a moment to review. In this chapter, we:

- Provided a rationale for using a broad time period lesson plan in your thematic course
- Used our lesson on Black American voting rights to model the elements of a broad thematic lesson plan

CLASSROOM TOOL: Blank Lesson Plan Template

Lesson Title:	Time Required:

Unit Title:

Content Standard(s):	

Course Big-Picture Question:	
Unit-Level Focus Question:	
Lesson Focus Question:	
Learning Objective:	

Historical Content	Instructional Strategy and Sources

Historical Thinking	Inclusion and Engagement Element

Assessment: How do you know that students have achieved the learning objective?	
Modifications/Accommodations: How can you provide the necessary modifications or accommodations for special education/English language learner students to achieve the learning objective?	

FIGURE 5.20 Classroom Tool: Blank Lesson Plan Template

THEMATIC TEACHING IN ACTION
Narrow Time Period Lesson on Women and the War Effort

NOW THAT WE HAVE TAKEN YOU THROUGH A LESSON that spans a broad period of time, we will walk you through a narrow time period lesson. This second approach is likely the one that you are more familiar with—designing a lesson that covers a more discrete period. If you have been teaching for years, you might be reassured that you can use many of your tried-and-true lessons even in a thematic course! Most of your lessons probably cover one topic in one period, say the Treaty of Versailles or the Cuban Missile Crisis. In fact, many of our lessons cover a narrow period, and many of them were ones we had previously taught in our chronological courses. It is the *placement* of those lessons within your thematic unit that will be essential for your students to be able to make connections over time.

Building a Lesson That Focuses on a Narrow Period of Time

As mentioned previously, the narrow period lesson is one that you are probably more familiar with creating as they focus on one single event or topic. Though you may have these lessons at hand, it is important to consider the *placement* of these more traditional lesson plans in a thematic unit. In this chapter, we dive into our lesson on women and the war effort from our "Women and LGBTQIA+ Rights" unit. Before we get into the lesson itself, look at our unit map to see where we placed it in our broader unit (see Figure 6.1).

As you can see from our unit map, this thematic unit follows the history of women and the LGBTQIA+ community chronologically throughout history, covering many topics you would teach in a traditional U.S. history course. You might even have a lesson on women during World War II as we have highlighted in Figure 6.1. In a chronological course, however, a lesson on women's roles during the war would be part of a unit on World War II, and it would be placed between lessons on the Atlantic Theater and the atomic bombing of Japan. That placement would certainly make sense in a conventional course, but the topic of women in wartime often becomes an aside rather than the focus and is out of context

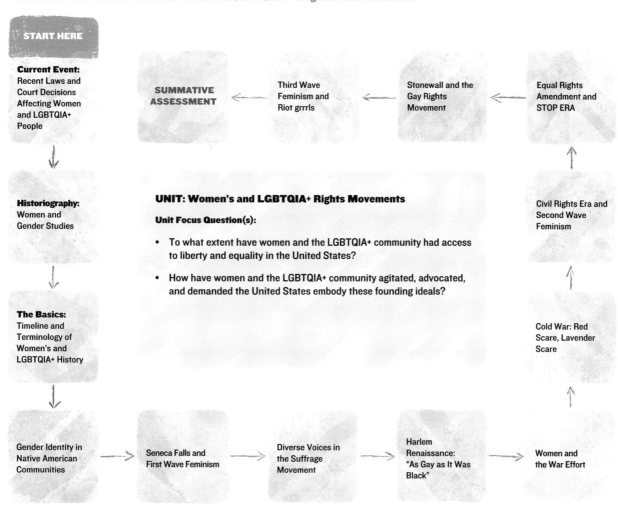

FIGURE 6.1 Thematic Unit Map: "Women's and LGBTQIA+ Rights Movements"

with a broader women's movement. Placing a lesson on a historically marginalized group within a broader unit on that group allows students to explore the cause-and-effect relationships more effectively between events since that is the *focus* of the unit, and not just supplemental to it.

In addition to placing our more traditional lessons around our unit themes, when modifying existing lessons to fit a thematic course, we asked ourselves which of our essential ingredients might be missing. Does each lesson plan use an inquiry-based approach, engage students with current events, and center identity and inclusion? We used our lesson plan template to ensure we captured all the ingredients, so our lessons will be engaging and relevant for our students. Whether the lesson spans a broad period, like the voting rights lesson we just examined, or a narrow time, like this lesson on women during World War II, we use the same lesson plan template, as it ensures *all* our lessons use an inquiry-based approach, elements of inclusion and engagement, and assessments and accommodations to provide checks for student understanding. Along with dissecting the lesson plan in this chapter, we examine the student handout to illustrate how students engage with this material. Because this type of lesson plan is one with which you are more familiar, we will move through it a little more quickly, highlighting the elements that we think are essential to the thematic approach.

An Overview of the Women and the War Effort Lesson

Like we did in our lesson from the previous chapter, we have provided a sample lesson plan and student document (see Figures 6.2 and 6.3). In this lesson, students examine the various roles women held during World War II and analyze how wartime propaganda encouraged those new roles. We always try to engage student interest at the start of a lesson by making connections to the present day; in this instance, students read an article (Spindel and Ralston 2021) and weigh arguments as to whether women should be drafted into the U.S. military. Then we draw upon students' prior knowledge about the Second World War. Students then engage in art analysis of Norman Rockwell's interpretation of Rosie the Riveter. After their examination of Rockwell's piece, students are tasked with finding their own World War II visual primary source that encouraged women's participation in the war effort, connecting their image to our theme of liberty and equality. As a lesson extension, students could watch and discuss the short documentary "Rosie the Riveter: Real Women Workers in World War II" (Library of Congress 2009) to gain greater insight into the contributions of women in the war effort and the legacy those efforts had on women in the United States.

LESSON PLAN

Lesson Title: Women and the War Effort	**Time Required:** 60 minutes

Unit Title: Women's and LGBTQIA+ Rights Movements

Content Standard(s):	**11.7 Students analyze America's participation in World War II.** 5. Discuss the constitutional issues and impact of events on the U.S. home front, including the internment of Japanese Americans and the restrictions on German and Italian resident aliens; the response of the administration to Hitler's atrocities against Jews and other groups; the roles of women in military production; and the roles and growing political demands of African Americans.
Course Big-Picture Question:	✳ How have historically marginalized groups agitated, advocated, and demanded the United States embody its founding ideals of liberty and equality? ✳ Evaluate the extent to which various groups were successful in attaining their rights to liberty and equality.
Unit-Level Focus Question:	✳ To what extent have women and the LGBTQIA+ community had access to liberty and equality in the United States? ✳ How have women and the LGBTQIA+ community agitated, advocated, and demanded the United States embody these founding ideals?
Lesson Focus Question:	How did World War II afford women the opportunity to gain greater access to liberty and equality? How did wartime propaganda encourage women to participate in the war effort?
Learning Objective:	Students will be able to address the learning focus question using both historical content and the historical thinking skill of cause and effect.

Historical Content	Instructional Strategy and Sources
✳ Causes and course of the Second World War ✳ Context of women in the workforce before and during the war ✳ The role and strategies of wartime propaganda ✳ Military and domestic production roles of women during the war	✳ Art analysis of Norman Rockwell's *Saturday Evening Post* cover of Rosie from May 29, 1943 ✳ Research and analysis of World War II propaganda urging women into the war effort ✳ Library of Congress video "Rosie the Riveter: Real Women Workers in World War II" (extension)

Historical Thinking	Inclusion and Engagement Element
Cause and effect Visual primary source analysis	Opening question about women and the present-day draft (*Washington Post* article "Congress Might Require Women to Register for the Draft" from November 15, 2021) Centering lesson on women during World War II

Assessment: How do you know that students have achieved the learning objective?	Students will post on a virtual whiteboard to share their art analysis findings. Students will research wartime propaganda targeting women and use it to address the lesson focus questions. Strong responses will cite specific historical evidence and draw clear connections to explain how World War II expanded opportunities and encouraged women's participation.
Modifications/Accommodations: How can you provide the necessary modifications or accommodations for special education/English language learner students to achieve the learning objective?	All of the following will be provided as needed: ✳ Extended time for activity ✳ Sentence starters for written responses ✳ Option for verbal response as opposed to written ✳ Partner work for the formative assessment

FIGURE 6.2 Sample Lesson Plan for Teachers: Narrow Time Period

WOMEN AND THE WAR EFFORT

CONNECTING WITH THE PAST
⁎ **Pair Share:** Should women be required to register for the draft for service in the armed forces? Read the *Washington Post* article titled "Congress Might Require Women to Register for the Draft. Where Do Republicans and Democrats Stand?" and make an argument using evidence from the source.

LESSON FOCUS QUESTIONS: How did World War II afford women the opportunity to gain greater access to liberty and equality? How did wartime propaganda encourage women to participate in the war effort?

DRAWING ON STUDENTS' PRIOR KNOWLEDGE
⁎ What do you remember about World War II from our previous units?

FIGURE 6.3 Sample Lesson Plan for Students: Narrow Time Period *(continues)*

In the chart below, describe what you see, and then explain what you think it means. Prepare your responses on this document, and then post your findings on the virtual whiteboard.

Describe what you see in the image:	Explain what you think it means:

What questions come up for you?

How does this image help you explain how World War II afforded women the opportunity to gain greater access to liberty and equality? How does the image encourage women to participate in the war effort?

FORMATIVE ASSESSMENT: RESEARCH ACTIVITY

❋ Using the internet, locate a visual primary source (poster art or photograph) of wartime propaganda targeting women as the audience.

On a separate sheet of paper, analyze the selected document by performing the steps above for the selected source: Describe elements of the poster or photograph and explain its meaning. Next, use clear and complete sentences to respond to both lesson focus questions: How does the image help you explain how World War II afforded women the opportunity to gain greater access to liberty and equality? How does the image encourage women to participate in the war effort? Your responses will be evaluated for use of specific evidence and clarity of explanations of how World War II expanded opportunities and encouraged women's participation.

LESSON EXTENSION: Watch the documentary "Rosie the Riveter: Real Women Workers in World War II" on YouTube for more information about Rockwell's work and the contributions of women during the war.

FIGURE 6.3 *(continued)* Sample Lesson Plan for Students: Narrow Time Period

Now that we have an overview of the lesson, we will break down each component in more detail.

An Inquiry-Based Approach: Women and the War Effort

Just as we did in our voting rights lesson, we begin by identifying which content standard(s) this lesson will address. It is important to consider what a school, district, or state requires students to learn in our classes. However, not every site has these learning standards. Many states, including California, where we teach, task public school teachers with teaching the contributions and roles of various groups of U.S. citizens on the home front during World War II. Although the state standard in Figure 6.4 includes the experiences of many U.S. citizens and residents, our lesson focuses on the role of women. The other elements of the standard will be covered in units relevant to those topics. Consider this approach when examining your own required standards, if you have them. Try to examine such standards through the lens of each of the unit themes you created in Chapter 2. Part of a standard might fit in your thematic unit on foreign policy, and another part of the standard could be more appropriate for a unit on new technologies.

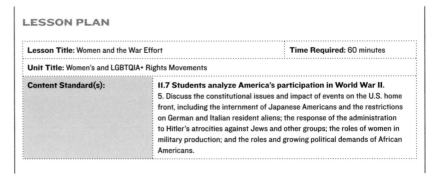

LESSON PLAN

Lesson Title: Women and the War Effort	**Time Required:** 60 minutes
Unit Title: Women's and LGBTQIA+ Rights Movements	

Content Standard(s):	**II.7 Students analyze America's participation in World War II.** 5. Discuss the constitutional issues and impact of events on the U.S. home front, including the internment of Japanese Americans and the restrictions on German and Italian resident aliens; the response of the administration to Hitler's atrocities against Jews and other groups; the roles of women in military production; and the roles and growing political demands of African Americans.

FIGURE 6.4 Sample Lesson Plan and Content Standards for Teachers

To engage students in historical inquiry and connect to our unit-level questions, our lesson focus questions ask students how the Second World War served as a means for women to gain greater access to liberty and equality, and how wartime propaganda encouraged their participation (see Figure 6.5). Although a teacher could simply ask students to identify what new roles women held in wartime, that question would not leave room for students to meaningfully engage with the material, nor does it connect to our course theme. Our lesson focuses on questions that ask students to think as historians, uncovering the cause-and-effect relationship between women's war efforts and the impact those efforts had on women's access to liberty and equality. Remember, by successfully answering the lesson focus questions, students are building a foundation to be able to answer the unit-level focus questions by the end of the thematic unit.

Course Big-Picture Question:	* How have historically marginalized groups agitated, advocated, and demanded the United States embody its founding ideals of liberty and equality? * Evaluate the extent to which various groups were successful in attaining their rights to liberty and equality.
Unit-Level Focus Question:	* To what extent have women and the LGBTQIA+ community had access to liberty and equality in the United States? * How have women and the LGBTQIA+ community agitated, advocated, and demanded the United States embody these founding ideals?
Lesson Focus Question:	How did World War II afford women the opportunity to gain greater access to liberty and equality? How did wartime propaganda encourage women to participate in the war effort?
Learning Objective:	Students will be able to address the learning focus question using both historical content and the historical thinking skill of cause and effect.

FIGURE 6.5 Sample Lesson Plan and Inquiry-Based Approach for Teachers

The final part of this section of the lesson plan is the learning objective (see Figure 6.5). Here, we ask that students address the learning focus question using both historical content and the historical thinking skill of cause and effect. We want students to see the roles women played in the Second World War—how they affected the course of the global conflict as key participants and how their lives were changed as a result. Also, we want to highlight causal connections within the narrow lesson plan and across the entire thematic unit.

Elements of the Thematic Lesson: Women and the War Effort

After determining our lesson questions and objective, we unpack the elements of this thematic lesson that help support students in their historical inquiry. We always consider what historical content students will need to know to answer the lesson-focused question (see Figure 6.6).

We want students to understand the causes and course of World War II for this lesson. Additionally, because the lesson asks students to examine *new* roles for women, students would need to have some knowledge about the extent to which women participated in the workforce prior to the war. This might include a recap or brief introduction of women's participation in past wars; the various job opportunities that were open to women in the nineteenth century, dependent on race and class; and the effects the Great Depression had on women in the workforce. Through the course of the lesson, students discover various military and domestic roles held by women during the war, including their work in the defense industries, their service as medical professionals, and their contributions in the U.S. Armed Forces. Additionally, their image analysis and research will help them discover the roles and strategies of wartime propaganda, including the theme of patriotism that is evident in so many of the images from this era.

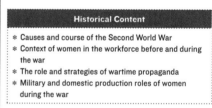

Historical Content

* Causes and course of the Second World War
* Context of women in the workforce before and during the war
* The role and strategies of wartime propaganda
* Military and domestic production roles of women during the war

FIGURE 6.6 Historical Content: Lesson on Women and the War Effort

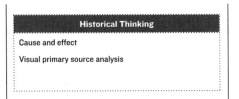

Historical Thinking
Cause and effect
Visual primary source analysis

FIGURE 6.7 Historical Thinking Skills: Lesson on Women and the War Effort

Inclusion and Engagement Element
Opening question about women and the present-day draft (*Washington Post* article "Congress Might Require Women to Register for the Draft" from November 15, 2021)
Centering lesson on women during World War II

FIGURE 6.8 Inclusion and Engagement: Lesson on Women and the War Effort

Both of our lesson focus questions ask students to engage in the historical thinking skill of identifying cause-and-effect relationships: How did World War II [cause] afford women the opportunity to gain greater access to liberty and equality [effect]? How did wartime propaganda [cause] encourage women to participate in the war effort [effect]? Additionally, students will analyze various primary sources through this lesson, including the Rosie the Riveter image we provide and the visual they find on their own (see Figure 6.7). Providing students opportunities to analyze primary source images, as opposed to only textual documents like in our voting rights lesson, gives students who may struggle with reading greater access to the historical content. Frequently, students can learn visually through pieces of art, maps, and political cartoons to better grasp a concept or idea once they see it. It is important to keep in mind the types of primary sources included in your lesson to best support the historical thinking skill you are asking students to use.

Our next lesson plan element is focused on inclusion and engagement (see Figure 6.8). For this lesson, we try to garner student interest from the start by having students read a news article and discuss the present-day debate over women being drafted into the military. This topic directly connects to our historical lesson and our course theme, and it is one that piques students' interest as they will soon register to vote and be of a draftable age. After providing students time to share their thoughts with a partner, we use a Four Corners debate strategy that gets students moving into one of four corners in the classroom, depending on whether they strongly agree, agree, disagree, or strongly disagree with our provocative statement: *Women should be required to register for the draft for service in the armed forces* (see Figure 6.9). Not only are we engaging students in a topic that interests them, but we are tapping into kinesthetic learning by getting them up and moving. This opening activity makes the lesson more student centered as it values their voices in the discussion. Once students see the relevance of an issue to their own lives, they are much more likely to meaningfully engage in the history behind that issue.

WOMEN AND THE WAR EFFORT

CONNECTING WITH THE PAST
* **Pair Share:** Should women be required to register for the draft for service in the armed forces? Read the *Washington Post* article titled "Congress Might Require Women to Register for the Draft. Where Do Republicans and Democrats Stand?" and make an argument using evidence from the source.

FIGURE 6.9 Sample Lesson Prompt for Students: Connecting with the Past

In addition to engaging students in the present day, this lesson is centered around the roles of women. As discussed earlier in this chapter, by placing this lesson in a broader thematic unit on women and the LGBTQIA+ community, rather than being situated in a unit organized around a particular time, the history of gender expression and identity becomes fully integrated into the historical narrative. Our lessons become much more inclusive of our student populations than is typical in a chronological course.

Besides considering ways to create a more inclusive and engaging lesson, we determine the types of instructional strategies and sources for the lesson. After engaging students in a discussion about women's present-day roles in the military, we draw upon students' prior knowledge about World War II. Once we establish a foundational understanding of the war, we move on to the primary source document analysis, which is the key instructional strategy for this lesson (see Figure 6.10).

When examining visual sources, we often see students take one of two approaches. Some students jump to analysis rather than taking the time to identify the details of the piece. This may lead them to misinterpret the message the artist is trying to convey. To understand the meaning of art or political cartoons, students must first be tasked with describing what they see. Students can then use those details as *evidence* from the document to support their analysis of it and correctly interpret the source. Other students may opt out of the activity, thinking they do not know what the image means at first glance. But by breaking down the process and having them begin by identifying the details in the piece, all students feel they have something to contribute, and they are building the foundation for analyzing the source. This strategy gives students the confidence they need to analyze these types of documents.

To implement this strategy, we had students complete the graphic organizer in Figure 6.11 to describe what they see, explain what they think it means, record any questions they have, and make some preliminary connections to our lesson focus question.

Instructional Strategy and Sources
✳ Art analysis of Norman Rockwell's *Saturday Evening Post* cover of Rosie from May 29, 1943
✳ Research and analysis of World War II propaganda urging women into the war effort
✳ Library of Congress video "Rosie the Riveter: Real Women Workers in World War II" (extension)

FIGURE 6.10 Instructional Strategy and Sources: Lesson on Women and the War Effort

Describe what you see in the image:	Explain what you think it means:
What questions come up for you?	
How does this image help you explain how World War II afforded women the opportunity to gain greater access to liberty and equality? How does the image encourage women to participate in the war effort?	

FIGURE 6.11 Sample Lesson Prompt for Students: Analyzing a Visual Source

We selected Norman Rockwell's 1943 *Saturday Evening Post* image of *Rosie the Riveter* (Norman Rockwell Museum), as it is an engaging visual source for students to analyze and can supplement the textbook's descriptions of women's roles during wartime. Images of women defying traditional norms recur throughout this thematic unit and is one way to show how women advocated, agitated, and demanded greater rights. Once students had time to view and think about the image on their own, we used a virtual whiteboard to record students' descriptions and explanations of Rockwell's magazine cover. We did not initially tell students this was an image of the iconic Rosie the Riveter. First we had them only describe what they *saw*. After identifying the details in the image, we asked them to explain what they thought those images meant. Once students noticed details, such as the figure's masculine work attire and the heavy machinery in her lap, they were able to connect those features to women stepping out of traditional gender roles for the time and their contributions to the war effort. See Figure 6.12 for sample student responses.

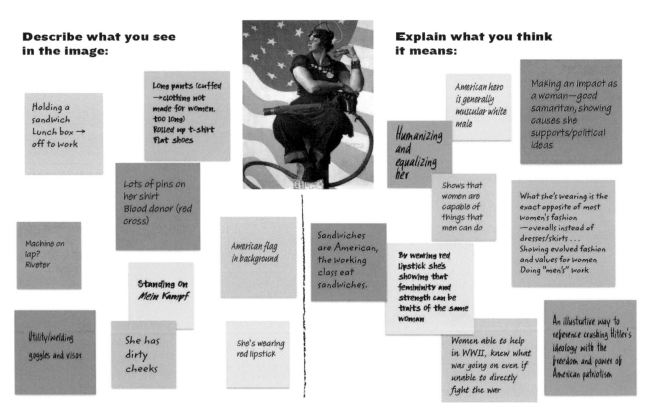

Describe what you see in the image:

Holding a sandwich Lunch box → off to work

Long pants (cuffed → clothing not made for women, too long) Rolled up t-shirt Flat shoes

Lots of pins on her shirt Blood donor (red cross)

Machine on lap? Riveter

American flag in background

Standing on Mein Kampf

Utility/welding goggles and visor

She has dirty cheeks

She's wearing red lipstick

Sandwiches are American, the working class eat sandwiches.

Explain what you think it means:

American hero is generally muscular white male

Making an impact as a woman—good samaritan, showing causes she supports/political ideas

Humanizing and equalizing her

Shows that women are capable of things that men can do

What she's wearing is the exact opposite of most women's fashion —overalls instead of dresses/skirts . . . Showing evolved fashion and values for women Doing "men's" work

By wearing red lipstick she's showing that femininity and strength can be traits of the same woman

Women able to help in WWII, knew what was going on even if unable to directly fight the war

An illustrative way to reference crushing Hitler's ideology with the freedom and power of American patriotism

FIGURE 6.12 Student Responses to Visual Source Analysis

Assessments and Accommodations: Women and the War Effort

Once students have analyzed and discussed Rockwell's *Rosie the Riveter* image, students then use the internet to find their own primary source image of wartime propaganda encouraging women to participate in the war effort. If your students do not have access to the internet in the classroom, you might provide additional resources that you have found and project them for students to see. Students use the same steps in the graphic organizer to analyze the image they found and respond to the learning focus questions.

This formative assessment is designed to give students practice in making a written argument based on the evidence they have collected. The assessment is connected to our lesson focus questions and our course theme, and it gives teachers a chance to assess the growth students are making toward our broader course goals (see Figures 6.13 and 6.14).

Assessment: How do you know that students have achieved the learning objective?	Students will post on a virtual whiteboard to share their art analysis findings. Students will research wartime propaganda targeting women and use it to address the lesson focus questions. Strong responses will cite specific historical evidence and draw clear connections to explain how World War II expanded opportunities and encouraged women's participation.

FIGURE 6.13 Sample Lesson Plan and Assessment for Teachers

FORMATIVE ASSESSMENT: RESEARCH ACTIVITY
* Using the internet, locate a visual primary source (poster art or photograph) of wartime propaganda targeting women as the audience.

On a separate sheet of paper, analyze the selected document by performing the steps above for the selected source: Describe elements of the poster or photograph and explain its meaning. Next, use clear and complete sentences to respond to both lesson focus questions: How does the image help you explain how World War II afforded women the opportunity to gain greater access to liberty and equality? How does the image encourage women to participate in the war effort? Your responses will be evaluated for use of specific evidence and clarity of explanations of how World War II expanded opportunities and encouraged women's participation.

LESSON EXTENSION: Watch the documentary "Rosie the Riveter: Real Women Workers in World War II" on YouTube for more information about Rockwell's work and the contributions of women during the war.

FIGURE 6.14 Sample Lesson Prompt for Students: Formative Assessment Research Activity

When discussing our voting rights lesson, we suggested some strategies for modifying the lesson to ensure it is accessible to all learners, such as providing vocabulary and sentence starters (see Figure 6.15). Those same strategies can certainly be utilized in this lesson. In addition, it can be helpful for teachers to consider how to meet the needs of students who move at a faster pace. In this lesson, we added an extension activity in which students can watch a short documentary that further analyzes Norman Rockwell's painting and briefly discusses the legacies of women's new roles (see Figure 6.16). The documentary could also be used to explain the meaning of the Norman Rockwell image more fully, which can be particularly helpful for students who benefit from extended time to process analytical information. The thorough debriefing of the image in the video can help to reinforce the analysis done by the students.

Modifications/Accommodations: How can you provide the necessary modifications or accommodations for special education/English language learner students to achieve the learning objective?	All of the following will be provided as needed: * Extended time for activity * Sentence starters for written responses * Option for verbal response as opposed to written * Partner work for the formative assessment

FIGURE 6.15 Lesson Plan and Modifications/Accommodations for Teachers

LESSON EXTENSION: Watch the documentary "Rosie the Riveter: Real Women Workers in World War II" on YouTube for more information about Rockwell's work and the contributions of women during the war.

FIGURE 6.16 Lesson Plan and Lesson Extension for Teachers

Not only are primary sources essential in the thematic classroom, but secondary sources also play a vital role. Secondary sources, such as the video by a historian for the Library of Congress (Library of Congress 2009), present broader context than one or multiple primary sources can provide. The video shows how diverse types of evidence fit together and compares several images, giving students an example of how historians engage with multiple pieces of historical source material. We use this video as an extension activity, but secondary sources can, and should, be used throughout a thematic course to provide historical context, to corroborate evidence from primary sources, and to model the skill of historical interpretation.

Putting It All Together: A Narrow Time Period Lesson Plan

Now that we have taken you through a sample lesson that spans a narrow period, practice designing one of your own. Remember, you do not have to create this lesson from scratch! Go back to one of the units you mapped in Chapter 3. Find a lesson topic from your unit map that spans a narrow period of time. Maybe you have an existing lesson on that topic that you could modify. If you are a new teacher and do not have prior lessons to pull from, you might start by choosing a topic you are most interested in—tapping into your interests as a teacher is important too! Once you have decided on a topic, walk through the steps outlined in this chapter to help you design a lesson that will be engaging and relevant to your students in your thematic course. Whether you are creating a new lesson or modifying one of your existing lesson plans, we encourage you to incorporate the thematic elements we have discussed: using an inquiry-based approach, engaging students through relevant present day and historical content, and including the experiences of historically marginalized groups. Use the blank lesson plan template provided in Figure 6.17 to create your own thematic lesson.

CLASSROOM TOOL: Blank Lesson Plan Template

Lesson Title:	Time Required:

Unit Title:

Content Standard(s):

Course Big-Picture Question:

Unit-Level Focus Question:

Lesson Focus Question:

Learning Objective:

Historical Content	Instructional Strategy and Sources

Historical Thinking	Inclusion and Engagement Element

Assessment: How do you know that students have achieved the learning objective?

Modifications/Accommodations: How can you provide the necessary modifications or accommodations for special education/English language learner students to achieve the learning objective?

FIGURE 6.17 Classroom Tool: Blank Lesson Plan Template

A GRADUAL TRANSITION TO A THEMATIC COURSE

Although some of you might be ready to jump right in and create a fully thematic U.S. history course, we know transitioning to an innovative approach can feel daunting. If you were concerned about the prospect of designing all new lesson plans, we hope we alleviated that fear by showing how you can use your existing lessons by simply changing the placement of them or making slight modifications to enhance their engagement and relevance.

If you are still not ready to fully transition, consider having a central, course-long theme that runs throughout each of your more traditional, chrono-logical units. For example, if your course theme is "What Does It Mean to Be an American?" you could examine each chronological unit through the lens of various groups' inclusion and exclusion in an American identity over time. Each unit could pose the thematic question at the beginning of the unit, then the question could be woven into the assessment for each unit. This approach might make you feel more comfortable following a common thread throughout the year until you are ready to develop thematic units that tie into that thread.

Another suggestion to help you ease into the transition is to begin each unit with a current event. At the start of your unit on America's Gilded Age, ask students if Amazon® is a monopoly and if it should be broken up. Have them read news articles arguing both sides of the debate. After they have examined the present-day issue of monopolies, students can dive into your unit and uncover some of the origins of this issue, including who benefits and who is harmed by economic conglomerations. Similarly, when beginning a unit on U.S. imperialism, students could examine the modern question of statehood for Puerto Rico, as we demonstrated in Chapter I. Starting the unit with an examination of a current U.S. territory will grab your students' interest from day one and allow you to focus a historical unit on the long-term implications of U.S. foreign policy, bridging the gap between past and present, which so rarely happens in a chronological course. This approach of starting each unit with a current event, although not fully thematic, still supports the goal of an engaging, relevant history course. ●

Chapter in Review

Let's take a moment to review. In this chapter, we:

- Explained our approach to creating a narrow thematic lesson by either designing a new or modifying an existing lesson that spans a narrow time period
- Broke down one of our own lesson plans on women's roles during the narrow time of World War II

ASSESSING STUDENTS IN A THEMATIC COURSE

In This Chapter, You Will:

- Learn about diverse ways to assess students in a thematic class, including the use of:
  - Written assessments
  - Project-based assessments

- Design an end-of-unit thematic assessment
- Create an end-of-year culminating assessment

BY THIS POINT, YOUR THEMATIC CLASS SHOULD BE STARTING TO TAKE SHAPE!
You have decided on your course and unit themes, mapped out the flow of your units, and created some engaging and relevant lesson plans for your students. The last step to rounding out your thematic units and your course is to develop authentic assessments so you can gauge your students' levels of proficiency at mastering the skills and content you have been teaching.

In previous chapters, we discussed assessing students at the end of each lesson as a quick way to measure your students' progress toward the learning objective. Those end-of-lesson formative assessments are great indicators to you that you may need to slow down the pace of the unit or make modifications to support student learning or that your students are ready to move forward in the unit. This chapter, however, will focus on summative assessments. Summative assessments are those that typically come at the close of a unit or the end of a semester or school year. Well-constructed assessments can inform teachers about students' progress toward content proficiency and historical inquiry. Additionally, assessments can provide authentic opportunities for students to dive into topics that interest and engage them, topics to which they feel a personal connection. In this chapter, we will demonstrate how to meaningfully assess students in a thematic classroom.

Since our lessons are centered around inquiry questions in a thematic approach, our assessments might look different from a typical exam in a chronological course. Chronological courses tend to focus on retaining information; thus, many traditional history courses utilize multiple-choice questions to assess student learning. We are not suggesting you do away with all your old exams. Multiple-choice questions can be a wonderful way to determine a student's progress toward content knowledge, and a well-crafted multiple-choice question can certainly call on students to use analytical skills. However, in a thematic course, our focus is on student inquiry. Each lesson is designed for students to act as historians and make their own meanings of the information we present to them. We are asking them to make connections between events and across time. We want to give them opportunities to express *their* interpretations of historical events and how those events impact the present day. Therefore, the assessments we use in a thematic course should not just ask students what they know but should give students the opportunity to *use* what they know to develop a historical argument.

Creating Engaging and Relevant Thematic Assessments

Before we go into the different assessment types, let's talk about what they have in common. No matter which types we are utilizing, we always want to ensure each assessment:

* Connects to our course theme
* Requires students to ground their responses in historical evidence
* Tasks students to use historical inquiry skills
* Taps into students' interests by offering opportunities for student choice

As we discussed earlier in the book, your course theme connects all the historical content, serving as a thread through which all your unit themes are tied. It provides a central focus for the course and was designed to be relevant to your students to fully engage them in the study of history. As such, your unit assessments should be *connected to your course theme* so students can see how each unit is part of a larger historical narrative. Connecting each assessment to your course theme will reinforce the key ideas you are trying to impart to your students. Students will not see the assessment as something they need to cram for the night before, only to forget the information after they complete the exam. Rather, they will see how the information from each unit works together to explore a bigger question, a question that helps them see the relevance to history and engages their curiosity.

Our job as history teachers is to ensure students learn history! Therefore, each assessment should *require students to ground their responses in historical evidence*. Students should have to cite specific, relevant, and accurate information in their assessments. This information can, and should, come from the various lesson plans you have taught throughout the unit or from independent research your students have conducted as part of your course. Students can pull from the variety of sources they have analyzed over the thematic unit. Historical evidence from primary source texts and images, secondary source materials, and textbook and lecture notes are resources they can draw from when completing an assessment. We certainly want to engage students through current events, and we want them to see how past events have impacted the present day. Therefore, your assessments might ask students to connect the past to the present day, as ours often do. But in a history course, the summative assessments should not focus solely on events that have occurred during your students' lifetimes. Be sure your assessments offer students opportunities to demonstrate their historical knowledge.

Each assessment should *ask students to use skills of historical inquiry*. Again, one of the benefits to switching to a thematic approach is that the focus of the course is on broader concepts or ideas, rather than the traditional march through history that we are all familiar with. To get students acting as historians and interpreting these broader historical concepts, we apply our inquiry-based approach to our unit assessments. Pose questions that ask students to consider the cause-and-effect relationships between events or across geographical locations. Have them consider how broader historical forces impacted a particular event or development. Ask them to examine how and why particular ideas or developments changed or stayed the same over time. They may also compare trends, processes, or groups, noting why similarities or differences occurred. When students see that *their* interpretations of history matter, they become much more engaged and invested in the content of our course.

To further student engagement, we think it is important that *assessments tap into students' interests by offering them some level of choice* in how they respond to the assessment. That is not to say that students can write about a topic of their choosing with no parameters. But just like you considered student engagement in your lesson plans, so too should you develop assessments that pique students' curiosity and allow students to play some role in the decision-making process. If you allow students some level of choice in your assessments, you will see how they dive

> "I saw more evidence of students drawing connections within units and across units than I have when I taught history chronologically. Why just the other day, I heard students comparing the sinking of the USS *Maine* with the Gulf of Tonkin incident and how they both started what they argued were unjust wars with Spain and Vietnam."
>
> **NICK** | teacher

deep into topics that are of interest to them. We will show you how our project-based assessments were designed with student engagement and choice in mind, but a well-crafted written assessment can also offer some flexibility for your students to demonstrate their understanding of the historical content in meaningful ways.

Whether you are designing a written assessment or a project-based assignment, we encourage you to incorporate all the tenets discussed here. As we go through each type of thematic assessment, we will highlight how we build careful connections to our course theme, require students to base responses on historical evidence, and ask them to demonstrate historical thinking skills. We also offer opportunities for student choice in the topics to address and types of evidence to incorporate in their final products. All four of these elements support the essential ingredients for a thematic course that we identified in Chapter 1.

Thematic Unit Summative Assessments

As history teachers, we want to know if students learned the historical content that we have taught them, but also if they understand the greater significance of that content. Whether a short response or a full, multiparagraph essay, written assessments provide students with the opportunity to demonstrate their proficiency of the skills we have centered in our thematic coursework. They can be designed to be engaging and relevant to our students and can get them thinking like historians.

When developing a written assessment for a thematic course, you should be reassured to know that you have already done most of the work for it as you have moved through the planning process in this book! Remember those unit-level focus questions you wrote in Chapter 2? Those questions were designed to be thought-provoking and elicit multiple responses. They allow students to utilize historical thinking skills, such as cause and effect or continuity and change over time. They span the length of your entire unit, and they are directly connected to your overarching course theme.

Let's look at our unit map for our "African American Freedom Rights Movement" unit one more time (see Figure 7.1).

We have two unit focus questions in the center of the map: To what extent have people of African descent had access to liberty and equality in the United States? How have people of African descent agitated, advocated, and demanded the United States embody these founding ideals? These are the questions your students have been working to uncover throughout the entire thematic unit. All your lesson plans were created

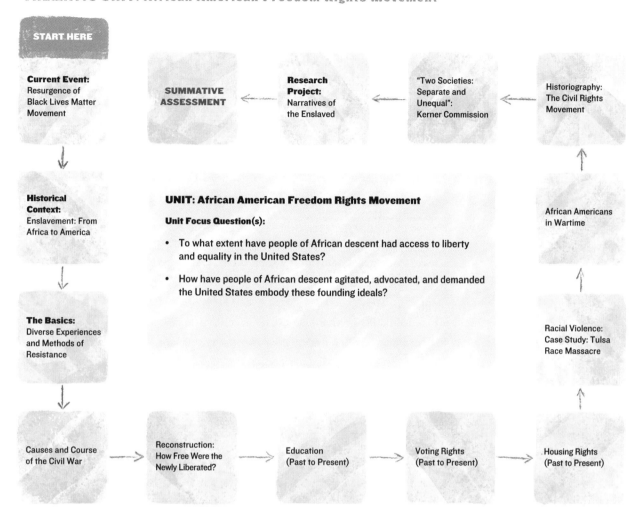

FIGURE 7.1 Planning Map for "African American Freedom Rights Movement" Thematic Unit

with these questions in mind. As such, they are a great starting point when designing your end-of-unit assessment.

For this example, we will show you one option of turning one of your unit focus questions into a potential short answer prompt. To make our assessment more feasible for students, we often modified our unit-level questions a bit to narrow their focus, setting clear parameters for students so they can write strong responses. For our "African American Freedom Rights Movement" unit, we posed the question seen in Figure 7.2 to our students as their assessment: To what extent have Black Americans achieved liberty and equality in the United States from the era of Reconstruction to the present day?

To what extent have Black Americans achieved liberty and equality in the United States from the era of Reconstruction to the present day?

In your response, use TWO of the following categories to support your answer:

- Education rights
- Voting rights
- Housing rights

FIGURE 7.2 Assessment on "African American Freedom Rights Movement" for Students

You can see this question is derived directly from one of our unit-level focus questions, but the time is defined, and we have selected specific topics we would like our students to address. We ask our students to write approximately one page in response to this prompt, a length that we think is reasonable and manageable for an end-of-unit assessment.

Even with the narrowed focus, the question still adheres to our tenets described earlier. It directly connects to our course theme, requires the use of specific historical evidence, and engages students in the skill of historical inquiry. If they choose to write about education, for example, they will certainly write about the *Brown v. Board of Education of Topeka, Kansas* (1954) Supreme Court Case, an important topic taught in most U.S. history courses. But rather than simply asking them to define the case, students could make their own historical argument about it, explaining how it advanced (or did not advance) liberty and equality for Black Americans. The prompt gets them to think deeply about the material covered in the unit. Additionally, the assessment offers students a level of choice, giving them the chance to show what they know. Perhaps they were particularly invested in your lessons on redlining and the impact those practices have on communities today. They can choose to write about the topic of housing rights and one other but can leave out the third.

If you find that when modifying your unit-level focus question, your assessment becomes too narrow and you want to evaluate students on other topics in your thematic unit, feel free to supplement the assessment with a more traditional multiple-choice, true-or-false, or matching section. Again, switching to a thematic approach does not mean you have to throw out all your tried-and-true materials! These more conventional assessments can be a wonderful way to assess students' content knowledge. However, we want our thematic approach to move beyond rote memorization and to be engaging and relevant for our students. Therefore, incorporating short written assessments becomes essential to putting our students in the role of historians.

THEMATIC TEACHING IN ACTION:
Short Written Assessment

Now we will walk through one of our short written assessments in more detail, providing sample student responses and a discussion on grading these responses. When designing our "Foreign Policy" thematic assessment, we considered our unit map, including our focus questions and the lesson topics that we covered throughout the unit (see Figure 7.3).

To narrow for a short answer response, we used our focus questions as a guide and reflected on the various lesson topics we addressed throughout the thematic unit. We edited one of our focus questions both in the periods of time students needed to address as well as the amount of evidence they were required to use in support of their answers. We decided on the following question to pose to our students to assess their

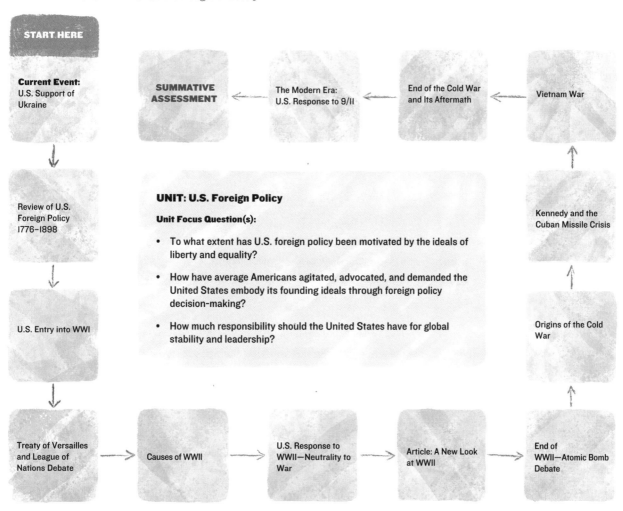

THEMATIC UNIT: U.S. Foreign Policy

START HERE

Current Event: U.S. Support of Ukraine

SUMMATIVE ASSESSMENT

The Modern Era: U.S. Response to 9/11

End of the Cold War and Its Aftermath

Vietnam War

Review of U.S. Foreign Policy 1776–1898

UNIT: U.S. Foreign Policy

Unit Focus Question(s):

- To what extent has U.S. foreign policy been motivated by the ideals of liberty and equality?

- How have average Americans agitated, advocated, and demanded the United States embody its founding ideals through foreign policy decision-making?

- How much responsibility should the United States have for global stability and leadership?

Kennedy and the Cuban Missile Crisis

U.S. Entry into WWI

Origins of the Cold War

Treaty of Versailles and League of Nations Debate

Causes of WWII

U.S. Response to WWII—Neutrality to War

Article: A New Look at WWII

End of WWII—Atomic Bomb Debate

FIGURE 7.3 Planning Map for "U.S. Foreign Policy" Thematic Unit

understanding of the unit (see Figure 7.4): To what extent has U.S. foreign policy been motivated by the ideals of liberty and equality?

> **To what extent has U.S. foreign policy been motivated by the ideals of liberty and equality? Support your answer using at least TWO specific examples between the Spanish-American War and today.**

FIGURE 7.4 Short Written Assessment on "U.S. Foreign Policy" for Students

Look at the excerpted student responses that follow. All four of the assessment elements we described previously are included in each response. Our course theme is woven throughout as students cite the ways in which liberty and equality have (and have not) been motivating factors for U.S. foreign policy. Additionally, each student uses specific, relevant evidence from our thematic unit to support their arguments, demonstrating their grasp of the historical content. They all use the historical inquiry skill of causation, explaining how and why the United States implemented various policies at different points in time. Finally, students' choice is represented in the events they decided to discuss. Whether they focused on the Spanish-American War or the Cold War era, many students cited evidence based on their own cultural background or personal interest. Students also had choice in their argumentation: while some asserted the United States had been motivated by the ideals of liberty and equality, others maintained less than lofty ideals were behind U.S. foreign policy decision-making.

> "While United States foreign policy initially was based on Manifest Destiny, it has overall been motivated by the ideals of liberty and equality through its support of democracy in struggling countries. . . . Later policy making moved away from the motives of Manifest Destiny and worked toward maintaining freedom in other countries. For example, the Truman Doctrine asked Congress for money in order to help European countries like Turkey who were fighting communist takeover. Also, the Eisenhower Doctrine announced that the U.S. would use force to help Middle Eastern nations being threatened by communism. Both of these policies were aimed toward preventing the presence of a very restrictive form of government. Communism effectively strips away the freedoms and equality that is offered by democracy, so the money from the Truman Doctrine was aimed at preventing the loss of those ideals in other countries."
>
> **Eva** | student

"U.S. foreign policy has partially been motivated by the ideals of liberty and equality, but often economic motivation and the pursuit of power has won out. . . . Americans may have fought for liberty at home, but they didn't extend that principle abroad. For example, during the Spanish-American War, the U.S. attained [*sic*] the Philippines, Guam, and Puerto Rico. Rather than establish liberty and equality or require consent of the governed, the U.S. used these territories to develop sea power. This pattern has persisted even in more recent history. During WWII, even though the U.S. opposed the totalitarianism and imperialism in Europe, the U.S. only entered the war when their territories were threatened, proceeding to ally with the USSR, a dictatorship."

Isabella | student

"Since its very inception, the United States has prided itself in being a nation guided by liberty and inalienable rights. Although the country's methods of extending these ideals weren't always justified, American foreign policy has demonstrated a great emphasis on freedom and democracy by countering nations with oppressive leaders and socioeconomic systems. . . . In the Spanish-American War (1898), the U.S. had the goal of 'civilizing' the Philippines. Spanish colonial rule would end in Puerto Rico and Guam, allowing the Americans to extend their influences and protect the territories from other foreign aggressors. In the next century, the U.S. would show their commitment to democratic liberties through involvement in the Korean War. As communist rule threatened to further impoverish and corrupt the country of Korea, the United States military recognized the failure of appeasement. These (and future) acts of containment ensured that communism wouldn't spread across all of Asia and strengthened the aggressive Soviet Union. Moreover, the United States had the preservation of their own domestic liberties in mind during the Cold War. Defense spending ensured that the world's global superpower remained one who strove for equity and peace."

Molly | student

In our thematic course, we want students to employ the skills of the historian: argumentation, use of factual details, analytical thinking. These skills allow students to demonstrate deeper understanding of the content, not just rote memorization. This makes written assessments an important part of our evaluation process. To facilitate the grading process, we use a standards-based grading rubric, scoring students on their thesis, use of evidence, analysis, and mechanics (see Figure 7.5). We introduce this rubric in our course syllabus, and we present it again prior to each assessment so students are aware of the grading criteria. As these criteria are assessed multiple times throughout the course, this rubric helps students chart their progress over the year on the historical inquiry skills we have been developing. For teachers, a good rubric can help manage the workload of grading written work. We can efficiently score their work using the rubric and provide a couple of short,

CRITERIA	Exceeds Standards	Meets Standards
Argumentation (Thesis)	Constructs a well-reasoned and clear argument in response to a prompt.	Constructs a clear argument in response to a prompt.
Use of Evidence	Uses accurate, specific, and relevant historical evidence to support an argument throughout the response.	Uses accurate, specific, and relevant historical evidence to support an argument.
Historical Thinking Skills (Analysis)	Demonstrates historical thinking skills—identifying historical context, continuity and change over time, cause and effect, compare and contrast—by consistently connecting historical evidence to an argument.	Demonstrates historical thinking skills—identifying historical context, continuity and change over time, cause and effect, compare and contrast—by connecting historical evidence to an argument.
Mechanics (Conventions; Creativity)	Produces quality work that is organized, legible/audible, and creative, depending on the task.	Produces work that is organized, legible/audible, and creative, depending on the task.

FIGURE 7.5 Rubric for Written Assessments *(continues)*

big-picture comments. In addition to students receiving our feedback and their score on the rubric, we often share examples of student work to demonstrate models of strong thesis statements, specific historical evidence, and solid analysis. Providing models helps students see there is not one correct answer we are looking for in their responses. This helps reaffirm to them that *their* argument, *their* interpretation of history matters.

CRITERIA	Approaching Standards	Below Standards
Argumentation (Thesis)	Argument is descriptive or unclear in its response to the prompt. Argument does not fully address the prompt.	Work lacks a well-reasoned and clear argument in response to a prompt.
Use of Evidence	Inconsistent use of accurate, specific, and relevant historical evidence. Evidence does not clearly, accurately, or relevantly support an argument.	Work contains evidence with major historical errors, is too general, or is irrelevant to argument. Work is missing evidence to support an argument.
Historical Thinking Skills (Analysis)	Inconsistent or superficial demonstration of historical thinking skills—identifying historical context, continuity and change over time, cause and effect, compare and contrast (describes rather than explains).	Work does not demonstrate historical thinking skills—identifying historical context, continuity and change over time, cause and effect, compare and contrast.
Mechanics (Conventions; Creativity)	The organization, legible/audible qualities, and creativity are not consistently demonstrated in this work.	Work lacks organization, legible/audible qualities, and creativity.

FIGURE 7.5 *(continued)* Rubric for Written Assessments

THEMATIC TEACHING IN ACTION:
Long Essay Assessment

Most of our assessments include a short response as described previously, but we try to incorporate at least one long essay response each semester to evaluate student understanding and to provide them the time to fully develop a longer answer to our central thematic questions. Although short student responses can be a manageable way to assess their learning at the end of a unit, opportunities to provide a longer written response help them develop the skills of constructing a multiparagraph essay and to fully formulate their ideas. Since most of the tenets of short and long written assessments are similar, we will simply dive into one of our long essay prompts and students' responses.

For our thematic unit on immigration, we used a long essay prompt that tapped into one of our focus questions on the extent that U.S. policies afforded immigrants rights to liberty and equality, and we required students to employ the reasoning skills of continuity and change over time. Unlike the short response assessments, we introduced the specific prompt on the first day of the unit. Students were told they would be writing a long response to the question as the assessment and needed to work through the problem as we learned the content each class period. To prepare for the essay, students considered evidence from each lesson and homework assignment to build an argument that addressed the focus question. Here is the long essay prompt we used (Figure 7.6): Evaluate the ways in which U.S. immigration policy has changed and remained the same from the late nineteenth century to the present day.

Evaluate the ways in which U.S. immigration policy has changed and remained the same from the late nineteenth century to the present day.

FIGURE 7.6 Long Essay Assessment on "Immigration and Migration" for Students

For each lesson, we incorporated a formative assessment that tied the day's instruction back to the big-picture question. This scaffolded approach helped students consider the ways that they might utilize the evidence and analyze how it addressed the prompt. Let's take another look at the map of the "Immigration and Migration" thematic unit we used in Chapters 3 and 4 (see Figure 7.7).

We used formative assessments throughout the thematic unit to prepare students for responding to the summative assessment. For example, at the end of the lesson on the Palmer Raids and the Quota Act of 1924, students were asked to consider whether these policies represented

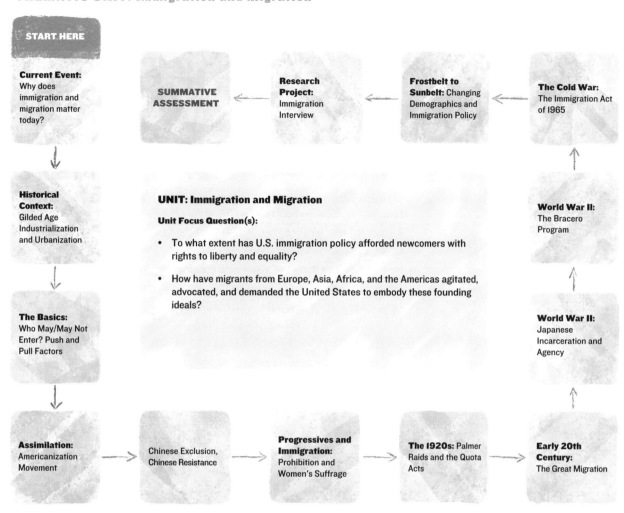

FIGURE 7.7 Planning Map for "Immigration and Migration" Thematic Unit

a change or continuation of previous approaches to limit immigration. In the lesson on the Immigration Act of 1965, students were asked to consider the same question, seeing how the 1960s legislation represented a reversal of country-of-origin restrictions but also continued a policy that provided caps on immigration and prioritized family reunification, which wrongly assumed immigrants would primarily hail from traditional ethnic stocks. Students used a simple T-chart to plot evidence they saw as supportive of a changing national immigration policy or a continued pattern in policies as they proceeded through the thematic unit.

Each of the following students' excerpted responses met the expectations from our assessment rubric: argumentation, use of evidence, historical analysis, and proper writing mechanics/conventions. For this assessment, they could build from their historical evidence and their thinking that they had captured in their T-charts to create and use a prepared formal outline with an argument, topic sentences, and specific details mapped out in advance. They had a full block period of 90 minutes to complete several multiple-choice questions, as well as the long essay response. This prompt could be amended for students on a modified curriculum to look at either continuity or change and require only two pieces of evidence to support their argument, like how we narrowed the prompts in our short assessment.

"Since its conception, the U.S. has struggled to define its immigration policies. A decade after its independence, the nation clearly expressed who it welcomed in the 1790 Naturalization Act, which reserved naturalized citizenship for white (Northern and Western European) immigrants only. This act set the foundation for centuries of discriminatory immigration policies that complicate the entry of immigrants into the nation and how citizens view newcomers. Although the U.S. has slowly been opening its borders to newcomers since the late nineteenth century, the nation's immigration policy continues to effortlessly restrict immigration on the basis of race and nationality damaging the economy and creating a nation of hate.

"U.S. immigration policy has become more welcoming over time, helping immigrants arrive and settle in the country. For example, the 1898 court case *U.S. v. Wong Kim Ark* legally acknowledged [Wong] Kim Ark's argument for citizenship at birthright. This ruling eased the doubts of families that had immigrated to the U.S., assuring their children would stay in the nation and be regarded as an equal under the law. The ruling also combatted the 1790 Naturalization Act, which implicitly resulted in the notion that birthright citizenship is reserved only for white immigrants. Overall, the ruling was monumental, and opened the borders of the U.S. to newcomers who saw the promise of a thriving land for their families. Nearly a century later, the 1965 Immigration and Naturalization Act eliminated immigration quotas set up earlier in the century. The U.S. immediately saw a boom in immigration from all over the globe. The act proved opening borders was phenomenal, as the newcomers created new economic opportunities and brought their cultures with them. Lastly, such openness toward immigration also thrives in modern times. The 2012 Deferred Act for Childhood Arrivals (DACA) allowed 'young unauthorized immigrants with low enforcement priorities to remain in the country with a temporary lawful status.' In effect, the act made it easier for immigrants to remain in the country as their children were protected under the law. Overall, the act raised the appeal for newcomers to settle in the U.S. In all, these three major policies over a span of hundreds of years have opened the U.S.'s borders and created a welcoming atmosphere for newcomers."

Hailey | student

"America has always taken pride in its large flow of immigrants and its tradition to welcome newcomers into the country. However, U.S. immigration policy is constantly changing. The Naturalization Act of 1790 stated only white immigrants who have resided in the U.S. for two years could become citizens. Policies like this redefine what it means to be a citizen, how to attain a green card, the path to citizenship, and naturalization processes. While the reasons for denying immigrants entry into the U.S. have been ever changing from the late nineteenth century to modern day, U.S. immigration policy is ultimately characterized by its continuous nature to forget and exclude people of specific races. . . .

"Although the changes in restrictions of immigration tremendously impacted U.S. immigration policy, the tendency for immigration policy to prey on certain races remains more prominent. America's immigration policy adopted many xenophobic acts such as the Chinese Exclusion Act of 1882. This act prohibited immigration of Chinese people, limited rights of Chinese already in the U.S., forbade naturalization of Chinese people, and prevented Chinese people from visiting their family due to fear of not being able to reenter. Clearly, this specifically targets one group of people solely based on their race and no logical reasoning. This pattern continues with the Immigration Act of 1924, which limited the number of immigrants allowed entry into the U.S. through a national origins quota. The quota provided immigration to 2% of the total number of people of each nationality in the U.S. This only allows a small number of people entry and is designed to keep races such as the Japanese and Chinese out of America. Furthermore, Trump's Travel Ban in 2017 continues to suspend immigration from certain countries. Trump called for the suspension of seven 'terror prone' countries including Iran, Iraq, Libya, Somalia, Sudan, Syria, and Yemen. There is no evaluation of moral character in this policy; the only reasoning lies in racism where there is an assumption that all people from these countries are dangerous. It can be seen again and again that immigration policy is adjusted to keep select races (mainly those that aren't white) out of the United States."

Carrie | student

These student responses present different interpretations of the course theme on immigration policy and examine the patterns of continuity and change over time. Although they incorporate and examine different evidence, they connect past events to more recent ones, showing how history still has relevance to people's lives today. Some of the students, whose excerpts are included here, are immigrants themselves or second generation in the United States, which allowed them to draw additional meaning from the unit and prompt. In a traditional history course, students would have had a greater challenge to make these connections and may have missed the broader arcs of change and continuity if the content were dispersed over several chronological units. The thematic approach for this unit effectively centered immigration, which is such a central aspect of the U.S. national identity.

THEMATIC TEACHING IN ACTION: Project-Based Learning

Although many of our thematic units end with a written assessment, we try to incorporate project-based assessments throughout the year. We find that although many students can successfully demonstrate their proficiency in the content and historical thinking skills through writing, others perform better when they are afforded the opportunity to tap into their creativity in a different way. Project-based assessments can be an engaging and innovative way to evaluate student learning in a thematic course. They can be rigorous and require students to demonstrate their depth of historical knowledge while allowing students to convey that knowledge in an alternative way.

You are probably familiar with project-based learning and its benefits in a history classroom. If you have been teaching for years, you likely have your favorite projects that intrigue students each year. Just as we discussed with written assessments, you do not need to retire all your successful projects. But creating a thematic course might be a terrific opportunity for you to develop projects that allow students to trace ideas and developments over time or that have a direct connection to the present day or that are driven by student choice.

Let's say you have a thematic unit titled "War and Diplomacy." Your end-of-unit project could ask students to choose a war and write a letter to the president, advising whether to consider a set of diplomatic actions prior to, or at the close of, the war. Students could base their proposed actions on actual historical events of the era, but students may examine those events through a new lens. If you have "The Impact of Art" as a thematic unit, students could choose a work that you analyzed in the unit and create a contemporary interpretation of it, explaining the choices they made in adapting the piece for the modern day. A "History Through the Lens of Sports" thematic unit could lend itself to a project in which students choose from a list of significant Olympic years and research how broader world events impacted certain Olympic games.

When creating projects for a thematic course, it is important to incorporate the same tenets as we use in our written assessments. Adhering to these components ensures that the project supports your larger course goals, is academic, and engages students so they do their best work.

Here, we will offer you an alternative end-of-unit assessment for the same immigration-based thematic unit described previously. Unlike the long essay prompt, which asked students to discuss broader policy decision-making, we wanted our students to dive into the topic of immigration on a more personal level. So, we asked our students to conduct an interview of someone who immigrated to the United States. This could be a family member, classmate, friend—anyone with whom they had a personal connection and wanted to know more about their story. We gave them a list of questions we wanted them to ask that tapped into many of the previous lessons in the unit. For example, they had to inquire about push and pull factors, whether they were part of a larger wave of immigration, and the interviewee's thoughts on how the United States had fulfilled its ideals of liberty and equality for immigrants. Our students also had to write their own additional questions and give space in the interview for the interviewee to share what they wanted to share (see Figure 7.8).

IMMIGRATION INTERVIEW/RESEARCH PROJECT

Step 1: Setting up and preparing for the interview

* Who are you going to interview? Preferably you can interview a family member, but also consider neighbors, classmates, teachers, coaches, community members, etc. If you are an immigrant, please consider allowing a classmate to interview you.
* Contact the person and set up a date, time, and location.
* Create a list of 5–7 questions to ask your interviewee in addition to the ones I've written.

Step 2: Conducting the interview

* Record and/or take notes on the interview—if you are interviewing a family member, consider video recording the interview. It could be a wonderful family keepsake. Be sure to get permission from your interviewee before you videotape or audio tape the interview.
* In addition to asking the questions you have prepared, feel free to ask additional questions during the interview as the conversation progresses. Let the interviewee take you where they want to go!
* You will submit your recording and/or notes.
* Be sure to thank your interviewee—a handwritten note goes a long way to express your gratitude!

Step 3: Researching and writing component

You will use your interview as a jumping-off point to do further research on the experiences of immigrants from the same region/country as your interviewee.
* *Part I:* One or two paragraphs summarizing your interviewee's story
* *Part II:* Two or three paragraphs providing historical background beyond your interview
  • Have there been waves of emigration from this country/region to the United States? When? Why? What was going on in that country/region that would encourage people to immigrate to the United States? What was going on in the United States that might make immigrants from that region want to come to the United States?
  • What common experiences did those immigrants have when they arrived/settled in the United States? Were they welcomed? Not? Which part(s) of the country did they move to?
* *Part III:* One-paragraph reflection: What were some of your takeaways from this project?
* Bibliography: MLA format, use of credible, academic sources

Step 4: Creating a visual of your interviewee's experience and the historical background you researched

You will share your visual with your classmates in small groups. You can do a poster or a slide. Your visual should include:
* A paragraph summary of your interviewee's story (can be pulled from your written component, but may be more concise)
* Meaningful quotes from the interview
* A paragraph of historical background (can be pulled from your written component, but may be more concise)
* A map/image of your interviewee's home country
* Perhaps a picture of your interviewee (with their permission)
* Other components that would be interesting or meaningful to convey

FIGURE 7.8 Immigration Interview and Research Project *(continues)*

IMMIGRATION INTERVIEW PROJECT

Step I—Setting up and Preparing for the Interview

Setting up the interview	
Name of the person you are going to interview:	
Your relation to the interviewee:	
Interview date and time:	
Location of the interview:	

Preparing for the interview

I have written a list of questions that must be included in your interview. In addition, you will write 5–7 questions that you want to ask your interviewee.

I. What is your country of origin? When did you immigrate to the United States?

2. Why did you leave your home country? (push factors)

3. Why did you choose to come to the United States? (pull factors)

4. As far as you know, were you part of a larger wave of immigration to the United States? (Were there many people leaving your home country at the same time for a particular reason?)

5. In what ways do you think the United States lives up to its promise as a nation that stands for liberty and equality for immigrants?

6. In what ways, if any, do you think the United States falls short of its promise as a nation that stands for liberty and equality for immigrants?

Write 5–7 of your own questions below. Perhaps you want to ask about their hopes, fears, challenges, etc. Jobs? Education? Memorable moments? Find out their story!

I.

2.

3.

4.

5.

6.

7.

FIGURE 7.8 *(continued)* Immigration Interview and Research Project

After students conducted the interview, they had to research the interviewee's country of origin and its history of immigration to the United States. This allowed our students to further explore many of the historical events we had covered throughout the unit in greater depth. Depending on the interviewee's home country, our students conducted research on the Irish Potato Famine, the Chinese Exclusion Act, the effects of the Holocaust, the Cuban Revolution, and Taiwan-China tensions, as in the student example in Figure 7.9. Students produced a written summary of the interview and detailed their research in a multiparagraph response. Additionally, they created a visual representation of their interview and research in the form of a poster or slideshow and shared their work with their classmates. By the end of the project, students had developed a deeper understanding of the history behind and present-day impact of immigration to the United States, not just from their own interviewee's home country, but from countries all around the world.

Just as in the written responses, students used a wealth of historical evidence, examined causation, and made direct connections to our course themes. Project-based assessments are an alternative way to have students make connections to the present day and practice skills of historical inquiry and often lend themselves to centering identity and inclusion. Our students appreciated the variety of assessments we have used since they can demonstrate their knowledge in multiple ways.

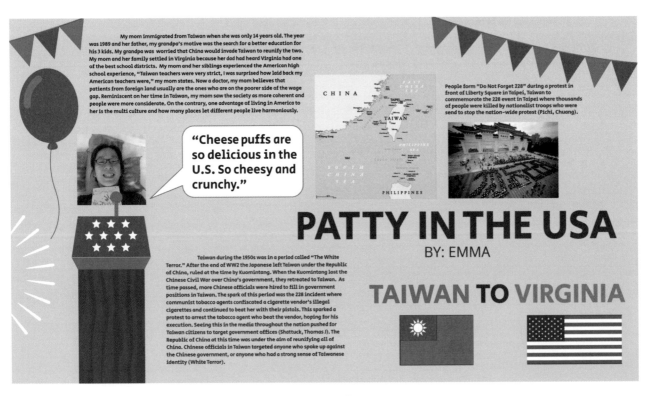

FIGURE 7.9 Sample Student Immigration Interview and Research Poster

Putting It All Together: Thematic Unit Summative Assessments

Now it is your turn! Here is a planning tool to help you develop a summative assessment for one of your thematic units you developed in the previous chapters (Figure 7.10). This can be a short response, long essay, or project-based assessment. Remember, your summative assessment does not need to cover everything from the entire unit. Focus on what is most essential, and feel free to supplement with more conventional multiple-choice, true-or-false, or matching questions.

PLANNING TOOL: Crafting a Summative Assessment

Look back at your unit-level focus question(s). What broad developments do you want students to demonstrate they understand?

Look at your thematic unit map. What specific events or topics do you want students to demonstrate they understand?

What historical thinking skills would you like students to demonstrate in the assessment? Is a comparison, change over time, or causation question most fitting for this unit assessment?

After noting the important content and skills for the thematic unit, craft a few written assessment prompts or questions in the space below.

Look at your thematic unit map again. Are there topics or lesson ideas that are essential but not reflected in the assessment prompt/question you wrote? Remember that you can always supplement the assessment with more traditional questions, such as multiple choice, short answer, true or false, etc.

FIGURE 7.10 Planning Tool: Crafting a Summative Assessment

Hopefully, the assessment prompt(s) you created incorporate all the tenets discussed in this section. Use the assessment checklist provided to make sure all the elements have been considered (Figure 7.11).

Do you feel that the assessment you created . . .		
Connects well with your course and unit themes?	_____ YES	_____ NO
Requires students to ground their responses in historical evidence?	_____ YES	_____ NO
Tasks students to use historical inquiry skills?	_____ YES	_____ NO
Taps into students' interest by providing opportunities for student choice?	_____ YES	_____ NO

FIGURE 7.11 Summative Assessment Checklist

End-of-Year Culminating Projects

Unlike most chronological history courses, thematic courses are organized around one course-long overarching central theme. All year, students work to uncover the intricacies and complexities of that theme while studying each thematic unit that supports it. A culminating end-of-year project is a perfect way for students to demonstrate their understanding of that theme. We want students to synthesize multiple pieces of information, make connections across time, and develop strong historical arguments, all while engaging in a project that is relevant to *them*.

Here are a few ideas for an end-of-year culminating project. If your central course theme is "We the People," an end-of-year culminating assessment could task students with choosing a group of people whose story is not traditionally taught in a typical middle or high school history course. Students could teach the class about that group through any medium they choose. They might opt to write a short, illustrated book to read to the class, create a minidocumentary, or compose an original song to perform for the class. If your course theme is "Ten Most Important Events" in United States or world history, a culminating project could have students choose which important event they thought you left out, research-ing the event, its historical context, and its legacy.

Like our thematic unit assessments, our end-of-year culminating projects adhere to our key tenets for a thematic assessment: connecting to our course theme, grounding in historical evidence, using historical thinking skills, and offering a level of choice to tap into student interest. In this section, we will walk you through our final project, explaining how we developed it and providing examples of student work. Then we will help guide you to developing your own final, culminating project—the last step to making your thematic class complete!

THEMATIC TEACHING IN ACTION: End-of-Year Project—Striving for Liberty and Equality

For our summative assessments, we started with our thematic map for each unit that we were assessing. However, our final project is not tied to one thematic unit; it is reflective of the entire course. Therefore, when designing our final project, we considered our course theme, "Striving for Liberty and Equality." All year long, our students have been acquiring the skills and knowledge to explore our two big-picture questions that support our course theme:

* How have historically marginalized groups agitated, advocated, and demanded the United States embody its founding ideals of liberty and equality?
* Evaluate the extent to which various groups were successful in attaining their rights to liberty and equality.

We wanted our students to explore how diverse groups of people used the founding ideals of the United States, as stated in the Declaration of Independence and the U.S. Constitution, to advocate that they be included in those ideals. As such, all our thematic units were designed with those questions in mind. Students learned how various groups have used their agency and activism to press for fulfillment of these fundamental rights, including Black Americans, immigrants, Native Americans, those residing in U.S. colonies, women, and the LGBTQIA+ community.

Of course, we wanted our final project to be meaningful and relevant to each of the students in our classroom. The final project had to incorporate student voice and student choice. Additionally, as part of our thematic approach, we were very intentional about connecting the past to today. We wanted our students to see that current laws, policies, practices, and events have their roots in the nation's past and that to understand the present, one must uncover those roots.

With all that in mind, for our final project, detailed in Figure 7.12, we had our students construct a visual timeline of U.S. history that intended to answer the question: To what extent has the United States embodied its founding ideals of liberty and equality between 1776 and the present day? Students chose two events from each of our seven thematic units that they thought best served as evidence to respond to the question. Recognizing the limitations of any survey history course in addressing all the topics students want to learn about, they had to present two additional important events that we did not discuss at any time during the school year. This was an opportunity for students to bring in historical evidence that was more personal to them and that reflected their priorities or values. On the day

US History Thematic Course: Final Project

Through the lens of our course theme, *Striving for Liberty and Equality*, we have spent this school year examining America's ideals as defined in the Declaration of Independence and the US Constitution -ideals of freedom, liberty, equality, and democracy. We have traced the history of various groups of Americans - African Americans, immigrants, Native Americans, US colonials, women, members of the LGBTQ+ community - to examine how they have agitated, advocated, and demanded the U.S. grant liberty and equality to all. We have also examined how the United States' economic and foreign policies have been in support, or opposition of the country's founding ideals. Now, using the historical knowledge you have gained this year, you will create a **visual timeline** that answers the question below.

> To what extent has the United States embodied its founding ideals of liberty and equality between 1776 and the present day?

Your Task: To create a **visual timeline** of U.S. history that emphasizes key events from United States history. Your visual timeline will be used in an end-of-year **fish bowl-style discussion** where you explain how these events each address the focus question above.

The Process:
1. Complete the graphic organizer by selecting TWO events from each module that you think best answer the guiding question. You should have FOURTEEN events, two from each of the seven modules.
2. Next, select TWO additional events that we did not directly learn about over the course of the school year. This part of the assignment allows you to explore something that you are curious about. At the end of your research, you should prepare to present SIXTEEN historical events on your timeline.
3. Then, create your visual timeline.
   a. The front of your poster should include the name of each event, the date(s), and a picture.
   b. Please color-code your events by thematic unit, so that it is easy to see how the events we have examined all year impact and interact with each other.
   c. The back of your poster will include a brief description of each event, written entirely in your own words.
4. Prepare an argument based on the evidence you gathered in your T-chart and prepare to defend your argument regarding ways the U.S. embodied the founding principles and ways that it did not do so.
5. On the day of the final, we will have a fishbowl discussion to develop responses to the prompt. You may use the timeline poster for reference to specific events, as needed. To be successful, prepare by explaining why you made the choices for your timeline and how they address the focus question.

FIGURE 7.12 Sample Thematic Course Final Project

of the final, students participated in a fishbowl-style Socratic discussion to reflect on the various events and patterns in U.S. history and the ways some had access to greater liberty and equality and reasons why others did not. Each thematic unit looked at events through a particular lens. This project allowed for students to synthesize a broader scope of U.S. history and to understand the forces of causation and correlation between events from those different thematic units.

To support them with this large project, we broke it down step by step, providing students with two weeks to complete the timeline and prepare for the fishbowl discussion. The graphic organizer shown in Figure 7.13 helped students keep track of their selected events, assured that they followed instructions, and provided a clear basis for them to formulate an argument in response to the question.

GRAPHIC ORGANIZER: VISUAL TIMELINE PROJECT

Thematic Units	Notes on the unit—Decide which two events are most essential from each unit to include in your timeline. Consider how each event demonstrates the embodiment of liberty and equality.	
	Events that demonstrate the United States has embodied the ideals of liberty/equality	Events that demonstrate the United States has not embodied the ideals of liberty/equality
Unit 1: Striving for Liberty and Equality		
Unit 2: Imperialism Across the Continent and Beyond		
Unit 3: African American Freedom Movement		
Unit 4: Immigration and Migration		
Unit 5: Women and LGBTQIA+ Rights		
Unit 6: Economic Justice		
Unit 7: Foreign Policy		
Select two additional events that you want in your timeline.		

FIGURE 7.13 Graphic Organizer: Visual Timeline Project for Students

This project allowed students to tap into their creativity and shine as artists and apprentice historians, showing what they learned over the school year. They had time to review their course content as they constructed their timelines. After examining the evidence, students developed their arguments, which ranged along a spectrum from those asserting that liberty and equality progressed to encompass more Americans over time to those contending that discrimination remained a prevalent feature of U.S. society. Students used diverse mediums and materials to create their timelines, from watercolor to graphite, and hand-drawn images to those sourced from the internet. They highlighted specific events in history from the drafting of the Declaration of Independence (1776) through the more recent *Dobbs v. Jackson Women's Health Organization* ruling (2022), and they used details to support their claims in a fishbowl-style discussion. Nearly all students chose their two additional events based on their own cultural heritage or gender identity, reinforcing the belief that students are more invested in the study of history when they see themselves represented in it. During the discussion, students were required to support ways in which the United States embodied the ideals of liberty and equality and the ways they did not. The assignment necessitated their understanding of differing points of view and to determine the best way to interpret this conflicting information. For a sense of how this project made an impact on students' understanding of our course-long big-picture questions, see students' comments and examples of finished products in Figures 7.14 and 7.15.

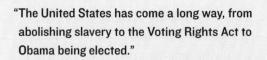

"The United States has come a long way, from abolishing slavery to the Voting Rights Act to Obama being elected."

Emma | student

FIGURE 7.14 Student Fishbowl Discussion and Close-Up of Jean's Visual Timeline

Tristan: "Should we praise the U.S. for its progress toward liberty and equality or is it an expectation that has already been written down and we should already be there?"

Dylan: "We should be praising the people who fought to *get* the government to make that change, like Frederick Douglass or Harriet Tubman."

Discussion between **Tristan** and **Dylan** | students

FIGURE 7.15 Image of Lynn's Timeline

For the assessment, we used our standards-based rubric (Figure 7.16), evaluating students' products, the timelines, as well as their quality of argumentation, use of evidence, and analytical thought demonstrated

CRITERIA	Exceeds Standards	Meets Standards
Argumentation	Constructs a well-reasoned and clear argument in response to a prompt. (Scoring is dependent on other skill criteria.)	Constructs a well-reasoned and clear argument in response to a prompt.
Use of Evidence	Uses accurate, specific, and relevant historical evidence to support an argument throughout the response.	Uses accurate, specific, and relevant historical evidence to support an argument.
Historical Thinking Skills (Analysis)	Demonstrates historical thinking skills—identifying historical context, continuity and change over time, cause and effect, compare and contrast—by consistently connecting historical evidence to an argument.	Demonstrates historical thinking skills—identifying historical context, continuity and change over time, cause and effect, compare and contrast—by connecting historical evidence to an argument.
Mechanics (Conventions; Creativity)	Produces quality work that is organized, legible/audible, and creative, depending on the task. The project completes all the necessary tasks.	Produces work that is organized, legible/audible, and creative, depending on the task. The project completes most of the required tasks.
Speaking	Speaks multiple times during the seminar without dominating. Provides ample support from the text evidence. Effectively contributes to moving dialogue forward by adding new thoughts/interpretations.	Speaks one to two times OR dominates the conversation. Uses text/evidence most of the time to support conversation. Contributes to moving dialogue forward.
Listening	Records thorough notes on discussion. Asks questions to clarify and/or build on what others say, Provides visual evidence of listening (sitting up, not "spaced out," no devices, or not doing unrelated work). Does not engage in side conversations.	Records notes on discussion. Provides visual evidence of listening (sitting up, not "spaced out," no devices, or not doing unrelated work). Does not engage in side conversations.

FIGURE 7.16 Final Project/Standards-Based Rubric *(continues)*

during the fishbowl discussion. Furthermore, we assessed their listening and speaking skills to make sure that all were fully engaged during the discussion.

CRITERIA	Approaching Standards	Below Standards
Argumentation	Argument is descriptive or unclear in its response to the prompt. Argument does not fully address the prompt.	Work lacks a well-reasoned and clear argument in response to a prompt.
Use of Evidence	Inconsistent use of accurate, specific, and relevant historical evidence. Evidence does not clearly, accurately, or relevantly support an argument.	Work contains evidence with major historical errors, is too general, or is irrelevant to argument. Work is missing evidence to support an argument.
Historical Thinking Skills (Analysis)	Inconsistent or superficial demonstration of historical thinking skills—identifying historical context, continuity and change over time, cause and effect, compare and contrast (describes rather than explains).	Work does not demonstrate historical thinking skills—identifying historical context, continuity and change over time, cause and effect, compare and contrast.
Mechanics (Conventions; Creativity)	The organization, legible/audible qualities, and creativity are not consistently demonstrated in this work. The project has incomplete parts, leaving out a lot of the required tasks.	Work lacks organization, legible/audible qualities, and creativity. The project is incomplete and/or off topic.
Speaking	Speaks one time. Doesn't use text to support ideas. May repeat previous points without providing new thoughts.	Does not talk during seminar.
Listening	Few notes are taken on discussion. Inconsistent evidence of listening. Engages in side conversations.	No notes are taken. Little to no evidence of listening. Engages in side conversations.

FIGURE 7.16 *(continued)* Final Project/Standards-Based Rubric

Chapter in Review

Let's take a moment to review. In this chapter, we:

- Discussed the use of two types of summative assessments in a thematic course:

  * Written assessments, both short and long responses

  * Project-based assessments, including:

    » End-of-unit projects

    » End-of-year culminating projects

- Highlighted four different tenets that each thematic assessment should incorporate, including:

  * A connection to the course theme

  * A grounding in historical evidence

  * Use of historical inquiry skills

  * A level of student choice to tap into student interest

- Examined four of our own assessments, including:

  * Short written assessment in our "Foreign Policy" unit

  * Long essay response in our "Immigration and Migration" unit

  * End-of-unit project in our "Immigration and Migration" unit

  * End-of-year culminating project (visual timeline and fishbowl discussion)

- Provided space for you to create your own unit and course-long assessments

Putting It All Together: End-of-Year Thematic Projects

We hope our example inspired some ideas for a final, culminating project that connects to your own course theme! You have already completed an incredible amount of work including developing course-long and unit-level themes and questions, mapping thematic units, creating lesson plans, and producing formative and summative assessments. The end-of-year thematic project is a great opportunity to tie all your work together. As you create your project, reflect on the essential ingredients of a thematic course: your personal why, centering identity and inclusion, and connecting to the present day to fully engage students in the study of history. Use the planning tool in Figure 7.17 to help you develop your end-of-year project.

Now that you have practiced creating written assessments and projects, either unit-long or yearlong, you have all the basic tools necessary to craft a cohesive thematic course. As you continue to develop the remainder of your unit assessments, we encourage you to take our important tenets and provide space for student voice and choice in the ways students demonstrate their understanding of the course content and skills. This will help engage your students more effectively and create the best opportunities for students to demonstrate what they have learned.

PLANNING TOOL: Crafting an End-of-Year Thematic Project

Write down your central course theme in the space below.

Write down your yearlong big-picture questions in the space below. You developed these in Chapter 2.

What historical thinking skills would you like students to demonstrate in their project? Is a comparison, change over time, or causation question most fitting for this culminating assessment?

How might this project center greater inclusion and diverse perspectives? In what ways is student voice and student choice presented?

After reflecting on your course theme and big-picture questions, brainstorm a few ideas for potential projects in the space below. What kinds of products do you want students to create that best demonstrate the big takeaways from the year?

Considering the historical content, thinking skills, and types of student products you brainstormed, choose one idea to develop for your final project.

FIGURE 7.17 Planning Tool: Crafting an End-of-Year Thematic Project

CONCLUSION

Our Reflection on the Thematic Approach

WE MADE THE SWITCH TO TEACHING HISTORY THEMATICALLY because our traditional, chronological approach was not meeting the needs of our students. Even with thirty-plus years of combined experience and pulling out every teacher trick in the book, we found that our students were often disengaged in the study of history, repeatedly asking us why they needed to know this or that. They wanted to know how history was relevant to them. And to be honest, we often had a challenging time answering that question for them.

Framing our course content around themes instead of time periods gave us the opportunity to structure our course in a way that connects to our students. As we have discussed throughout the book, we were more easily able to make connections from the past to the present day, providing our students with the answer to why the study of history matters to them. We were able to center the cultural, racial, and gender identities of our students in a way we could not do before. Every student got to see their own history represented in the course.

In addition, we found that the thematic approach encourages critical thought, whereas with the chronological approach, a teacher could simply tell the story of what happened. Our students' skills improved as we asked them to act as historians, investigating historical questions of inquiry. They engaged with the material we presented them in a much more meaningful way, solidifying their content knowledge and their ability to make connections across time and between events. They were able to trace a group or a phenomenon over an extended period of time rather than waiting for several units to return to that group, event, or issue, if at all.

Teaching history thematically truly allowed us to fulfill our personal why in the classroom. We created a course where students could see themselves in the curriculum. History was lifted out of the pages of the textbook and brought to life as students explored the lives and experiences of people like them. The connections we made from the past to the present allowed us to answer why students needed to know this history.

Our Students' Reflections on the Thematic Approach

Our students responded to our thematic approach with overwhelming enthusiasm. We surveyed our students at the end of each year. To date, 72 percent of our students reported that they preferred the thematic approach to the more familiar chronological approach, 18 percent said they had no preference, and only 10 percent would have preferred a traditional, chronological course. We asked them to comment on why they answered the way they did. Here are just a few of their responses:

> "[The thematic course] makes it so history isn't just stuff that happened hundreds of years ago but stuff I can connect to my life. I thought history would be boring but for the first time I've left feeling empowered."
>
> **Anonymous** | student

> "After looking at certain issues, I often google what is going on with the issue today. I want to know more about how our current society is dealing with issues that the society in the past dealt with."
>
> **Anonymous** | student

> "My parents and I are in awe of how amazing this course is because of how it teaches the real history and represents everyone. . . . I think the content of this class is so important and I wish that in the future, every history class is taught in this way."
>
> **Anonymous** | student

> "I wanted to express to you how impactful the African American history unit was for me. . . . Normally in history, these leaders and groups are only mentioned in the context of other, big events in U.S. history, and this totally diminishes their accomplishments/impact, so I really appreciate this course taking a deeper look at things."
>
> **Anonymous** | student

> "I really enjoyed the women's rights unit because usually leaving a history class I feel smaller and like all that was discussed is the negative. But this class was actually empowering and helped me understand all that's going on."
>
> **Sabine** | student

Through our students' responses, we clearly saw that the ingredients we identified as essential to a thematic course were making an impact. Students felt their identities represented in the curriculum, they recognized the connections we made to the present day made the class more relevant to them, and they felt like they were participants in the study of history rather than just receivers of information.

Student enthusiasm showed up in our classrooms in many ways. Students participated more. They asked more thought-provoking questions. They listened intently as their classmates shared their takes on a particular historical event. They came into our classrooms wanting to share how they did further research into the topic we were studying. They asked us for book recommendations, wanting to learn more about U.S. imperialism or the women's suffrage movement. Their writing improved as they wrote about topics they genuinely cared about, posing their own historical argument rather than simply regurgitating memorized facts.

Teacher Reflections on the Thematic Approach

Over time, more of our colleagues joined us on this journey. We have had opportunities to brainstorm ideas and share best practices with instructors within our own sites, district, state, and even across the country. The teachers we have worked with have seen results similar to our own as they developed their own thematic courses.

"Having an overarching theme for students to connect to within the thematic units was revolutionary. For the first time, I could see students making connections between the past and the present, as it was so easy to discuss the parallels of current events to the historical events we covered within the unit."

ALLIE | Teacher

"While this year was my first attempt at teaching thematically, I cannot imagine reverting to strictly chronologically. A thematic approach allowed me as a teacher to dive deeper into topics, whether focused on identity groups or major U.S. policy. Doing so gave my students the opportunity to see how policies and practices were simply rebranded or shifted away from one group onto another. This was the first year in my eight years in the classroom where I heard multiple students, each at different points in the year, say something to the effect of 'Oh, so this is just like what we did to Natives? I never knew that.' or 'Wait, that's exactly what happened with . . .' Those comments and similar feedback from students are why I will continue teaching thematically."

MATT | Teacher

"The students in my U.S. History Themes course were so much more engaged and connected to the curriculum as it took them beyond the scope of a regular U.S. history course, allowing them to learn more in depth about topics that they are witness to and or affected by in their day-to-day lives."

LYENNE | Teacher

Both new and veteran teachers we have worked with immediately saw the benefits of teaching history thematically. Just like in our own classrooms, their students were seeing the legacy of historical events on the present day, making connections across time in a way they had not done before. Teachers felt revitalized in the classroom, diving deep into topics that are often given short shrift. They also appreciated the flexibility to prioritize units or topics in the way they felt made the most sense for their students.

Final Thoughts on the Thematic Approach

We passionately believe teachers want to teach a class that is engaging, relevant, and inclusive of their students. So many teachers we have talked to said they have toyed with the idea of teaching history thematically but could not envision how it would come together. That is why we took our ideas and experiences and wrote them down in this book. We hope we have provided you with turnkey lessons and assessments, as well as the confidence and know-how to develop your own thematic course, making it your own. Everything in this book is available for you to use as is or to adapt to meet your own students' needs. Now that you have read our process and built the foundation for your course, dive back into different sections, rereading and reevaluating how to refine your thematic course, knowing that it will always be a work in progress, just as ours is.

Share these ideas and lessons with your colleagues. Build a professional learning community at your site that reexamines how history is taught. Teaching history thematically has the power to be transformative beyond the classroom. We know how important a well-informed and civic-minded citizenry is to the health of a democracy. The ability to think critically and understand historical forces are imperative to support a democratic society. History teachers are in a unique position to empower and inspire their students to become informed citizens, to help them see the relevance of history, and to provide opportunities for critical thought and expression. A thematic approach can better facilitate this by making history more engaging for students and by guiding their development of critical thinking skills. We hope this book has given you the know-how to develop your own thematic course, creating future generations of knowledgeable and engaged citizens.

APPENDICES

PLANNING TOOL: Your Personal Why

PLANNING TOOL: Crafting a Central Theme

What topics have you found to be engaging for your students in the past? What are some current events that might be relevant to the curriculum and engaging for students?

What are you excited about in studying or teaching U.S. history? What are some of your interests or passions that you might incorporate into a course theme?

Are there any historical works that you have read recently that have made a big impression on your thinking? Look back at your personal why from Chapter 1—what are some of your motivations for teaching thematically?

What words or phrases seem to recur in your state history standards? In your school's course of study? In your textbook? In your past course curriculum?

Have a conversation with a colleague in the Social Studies or English/Language Arts Department. What are some key themes they have used to explore their content with students?

PLANNING TOOL: Crafting the Big-Picture Question

What is your central course theme?

EXPERIMENT: Write at least ONE "how" question.

EXPERIMENT: Construct at least ONE "why" question.

EXPERIMENT: Compose at least ONE "Evaluate the extent . . ." prompt.

Final Question(s) or Prompt(s)

OR 4

Final Draft of Central Theme and Big-Picture Question(s) or Prompt(s)

YOUR FINAL DRAFT CENTRAL THEME

YOUR FINAL DRAFT BIG-PICTURE QUESTION(S) OR PROMPT(S)

PLANNING TOOL: Crafting Unit-Level Themes

Look back at your central theme and focus question(s). What major ideas and events would students need to understand to explore the theme and address the focus question?

What are you excited about in studying or teaching U.S. history? What are some of your interests or passions that could be incorporated into unit themes?

Look at your state standards or district course of study. Think about the essential standards you want to address. What (or who) is missing? List these below. Consider how they can be incorporated into your unit themes.

From the lists above, select the TOP ideas. Most units range from three to five weeks, so consider how much time you will have for each unit—this might determine how many units you have time to teach. These will be your potential unit themes!

PLANNING TOOL: Crafting Unit-Level Focus Questions

What is your first unit theme?
EXPERIMENT: Write at least ONE "how" question.
EXPERIMENT: Construct at least ONE "why" question.
EXPERIMENT: Compose at least ONE "Evaluate the extent . . ." prompt.
Final Unit Focus Question(s) or Prompt(s)

OR 7

Unit Theme and Unit Focus Question(s)/Prompt(s)

UNIT THEME	UNIT FOCUS QUESTION(S)/PROMPT(S)

PLANNING TOOL: Determining Essential Standards to Address Focus Questions

FOCUS QUESTIONS

TOPICS/STANDARDS TO ADDRESS	SPECIFIC DEVELOPMENTS TO ADDRESS

OR 9

PLANNING TOOL: Mapping the Flow of Your Thematic Unit

THEMATIC UNIT:

UNIT:

Unit Focus Question(s):

PLANNING TOOL: Responding to Your Own Thematic Focus Question

FOCUS QUESTION

YOUR RESPONSE TO THE THEMATIC QUESTION

CLASSROOM TOOL: Blank Lesson Plan Template

Lesson Title:	Time Required:

Unit Title:

Content Standard(s):	

Course Big-Picture Question:	
Unit-Level Focus Question:	
Lesson Focus Question:	
Learning Objective:	

Historical Content	Instructional Strategy and Sources
Historical Thinking	**Inclusion and Engagement Element**

Assessment: How do you know that students have achieved the learning objective?	
Modifications/Accommodations: How can you provide the necessary modifications or accommodations for special education/English language learner students to achieve the learning objective?	

From *Teaching Beyond the Timeline*. Portsmouth, NH: Heinemann. © 2024 by China Harvey and Lisa Herzig. May be photocopied for classroom use.

PLANNING TOOL: Crafting a Summative Assessment

Look back at your unit-level focus question(s). What broad developments do you want students to demonstrate they understand?

Look at your thematic unit map. What specific events or topics do you want students to demonstrate they understand?

What historical thinking skills would you like students to demonstrate in the assessment? Is a comparison, change over time, or causation question most fitting for this unit assessment?

After noting the important content and skills for the thematic unit, craft a few written assessment prompts or questions in the space below.

Look at your thematic unit map again. Are there topics or lesson ideas that are essential but not reflected in the assessment prompt/question you wrote? Remember that you can always supplement the assessment with more traditional questions, such as multiple choice, short answer, true or false, etc.

PLANNING TOOL: Crafting an End-of-Year Thematic Project

Write down your central course theme in the space below.

Write down your yearlong big-picture questions in the space below. You developed these in Chapter 2.

What historical thinking skills would you like students to demonstrate in their project? Is a comparison, change over time, or causation question most fitting for this culminating assessment?

How might this project center greater inclusion and diverse perspectives? In what ways is student voice and student choice presented?

After reflecting on your course theme and big-picture questions, brainstorm a few ideas for potential projects in the space below. What kinds of products do you want students to create that best demonstrate the big takeaways from the year?

Considering the historical content, thinking skills, and types of student products you brainstormed, choose one idea to develop for your final project.

WORKS CITED

Allen, D. S. 2015. *Our Declaration: A Reading of the Declaration of Independence in Defense of Equality*. New York: Liveright Publishing.

AllSides. n.d. https://www.allsides.com/unbiased-balanced-news.

Aspegren, E. 2021. "Kids Aren't Learning LGBTQ History. The Equality Act Might Change That." *USA Today*, March 8. https://www.usatoday.com/story/news/education/2021/03/06/lgbtq-history-equality-education-act-teachers/6648601002/.

Barton, K. 2005. "Primary Sources in History: Breaking Through the Myths." *Phi Delta Kappan* 86 (10): 745–53.

Biewen, J. (Host). 2017. "S2 E10: Citizen Thind." June 14. *Seeing White* podcast. Produced by Scene on Radio. https://www.sceneonradio.org/episode-40-citizen-thind-seeing-white-part-10/.

Brennan Center for Justice. 2021."Voting Laws Roundup: October 2021." October 4. https://www.brennancenter.org/our-work/research-reports/voting-laws-roundup-october-2021.

Brown University. n.d. "Choices Program." https://www.choices.edu/.

Brown University Choices Program. n.d. "Teaching with the News: Free Lessons Connect Your Classroom to Headlines in the News." https://www.choices.edu/teaching-with-the-news/.

California Code, Education Code – EDC 51204.5. Cal. S.B. 48 (2011, Amended 2023). https://leginfo.legislature.ca.gov/faces/codeBillCrossRef.xhtml?sectionNum=51204.5&nodeTreePath=2.3.4.3.1&lawCode=EDC.

California Department of Education. 2000. "History—Social Science Content Standards for California Public Schools: Kindergarten Through Grade Twelve." https://www.cde.ca.gov/be/st/ss/documents/histsocscistnd.pdf.

Daniels, R. 2019. *Coming to America: A History of Immigration and Ethnicity in American Life*. New York: Harper Perennial.

Densho Encyclopedia. n.d. "https://encyclopedia.densho.org.

Facing History & Ourselves. n.d. https://www.facinghistory.org/.

———. n.d. "Current Events in the Classroom." https://www.facinghistory.org/educator-resources/current-events.

Ferlazzo, L. 2020. "Seven Ways to Bring Current Events into the Classroom." Education Week, January 26. https://www.edweek.org/teaching-learning/opinion-seven-ways-to-bring-current-events-into-the-classroom/2020/01.

Ferris State University. n.d. "Jim Crow Museum—Question." https://jimcrowmuseum.ferris.edu/question/2012/pdfs-docs/literacytest.pdf.

Gay, G. 2018. *Culturally Responsive Teaching: Theory, Research, and Practice*. New York: Teachers College Press.

The Gilder Lehrman Institute of American History. n.d. https://www.gilderlehrman.org/.

Hammond, Z. L. 2015. *Culturally Responsive Teaching and the Brain: Promoting Authentic Engagement and Rigor Among Culturally and Linguistically Diverse Students*. Thousand Oaks, CA: Corwin Press.

Immerwahr, D. 2020. "History Isn't Just for Patriots: We Teach Students How to Understand the U.S., Not to Love It—Or Hate It. *Washington Post*, December 23. https://www.washingtonpost.com/outlook/2020/12/23/teach-history -american-patriotism/.

Ladson–Billings, G. 1995. "But That's Just Good Teaching! The Case for Culturally Relevant Pedagogy." *Theory into Practice* 34 (3): 159–61. doi:10.1080/00405849509543673.

Learning for Justice. n.d. https://www.learningforjustice.org/.

———. n.d. "Classroom Resources." https://www.learningforjustice.org /classroom-resources.

Lee, E. 2016. *The Making of Asian America: A History*. New York: Simon & Schuster.

Library of Congress. n.d. https://www.loc.gov/.

———. 2009. "Rosie the Riveter: Real Women Workers in World War II." February 10. https://www.youtube.com/watch?v=04VNBM1PqR8.

Loewen, J. W. 2007. *Lies My Teacher Told Me: Everything Your American History Text-book Got Wrong*. New York: Simon & Schuster.

———. 2018. *Teaching What Really Happened: How to Avoid the Tyranny of Text-books and Get Students Excited About Doing History*. 2nd ed. New York: Teachers College Press.

Los Angeles Times. 2015. "Selma 50 Years Later: Remembering Bloody Sunday." March 6. https://www.youtube.com/watch?v=Vn6uQBDAr_U.

Miranda, L., A. Lacamoire, and R. Chernow. 2016. *Hamilton: An American Musical*. Vocal selections. [Los Angeles, California], Warner/Chappell.

National Archives n.d. "Milestone Documents: Voting Rights Act (1965)." https://www.archives.gov/milestone-documents/voting-rights-act#:~ :text=This%20act%20was%20signed%20into,as%20a%20prerequisite%20 to%20voting.

Norman Rockwell Museum. n.d. "*Rosie the Riveter*—1943." https://www.nrm.org /rosie-the-riveter/.

Peters, T., Schubeck, K., and K. Hopkins. 1995. "A Thematic Approach: Theory and Practice at the Aleknagik School." *Phi Delta Kappan* 76 (8): 633–6.

PR51st. 2019. "Will Statehood Benefit Puerto Rico?" January 4. https://www.pr51st.com/will-statehood-benefit-puerto-rico/.

Spindel, J., and R. Ralston. 2021. "Congress Might Require Women to Register for the Draft. Where Do Republicans and Democrats Stand?" November 15. https://www.washingtonpost.com/politics/2021/11/15/congress-might -require-women-register-draft-where-do-republicans-democrats-stand/.

Stanford History Education Group. n.d. https://sheg.stanford.edu/.

Turan, I. 2020. "Thematic vs. Chronological History Teaching Debate: A Social Media Research." *Journal of Education and Learning* 9 (1): 205–16. doi:10.5539/jel.v9n1p205.

Zevin, J. 2000. *Social Studies for the Twenty-First Century: Methods and Materials for Teaching in Middle and Secondary Schools*. Mahwah, NJ: Lawrence Erlbaum.

Image Credits

Front Cover

Rosie the Riveter: Courtesy Library of Congress, https://lccn.loc.gov/2021669753
Voter registration: ©Everett Historical/Shutterstock/HIP
UMW symbol: ©Victoria Smith/Houghton Mifflin Harcourt/HIP
Bill of Rights: ©leezsnow/E+/Getty Images/HIP
Indigenous woman: ©Michelle Gilders/Alamy/HIP
Child: Library of Congress, Prints & Photographs Division, Farm Security Administration/
Office of War Information Black-and-White Negatives

Back cover

Statue of Liberty: ©VisionsofAmerica/Joe Sohm/DigitalVision/Getty Images/HIP
Child labor protest: Library of Congress/HIP
Author photograph: Jenna Wrobel

Interior

Page vi: Statue of Liberty ©VisionsofAmerica/Joe Sohm/DigitalVision/Getty Images/HIP;
Cliff Palace ©MarclSchauer/Shutterstock/HIP
Page vii: ©filo/E+/Getty Images/HIP
Page x: ©Victorian Traditions/Shutterstock/HIP
Page xii: ©Digital Media Pro/Shutterstock/HIP
Page xiv: ©Everett Collection Historical/Alamy/HIP
Page xv: ©Everett Collection Historical/Alamy/HIP
Figure 1.5: ©PR51st
Figure 2.4: Bobby Seale ©Archive PL/Alamy; Serena Williams ©lev radin/Shutterstock;
Pedro Pierluisi ©Ting Shen/Bloomberg/Contributor/Getty Images; Gladys Bentley ©FLHC
DBM2/Alamy; Malcolm X Courtesy Library of Congress, LC-USZ62-119478; Jackie
Robinson ©Hulton Archive/Getty Images; Marsha P. Johnson ©Diana Davies/New York
Public Library; Muhammad Ali ©Bettmann/Getty Images; Bayard Rustin Courtesy of
Library of Congress Prints & Photographs Division, LC-DIG-ppmsc-01272; Angela Davis
Courtesy of Library of Congress Prints & Photographs Division, LC-USZC4-7998; Gloria
Steinem Courtesy of Library of Congress Prints & Photographs Division, LC-U9-25332-25;
Constitution ©aristotoo/Stock/Getty Images/HIP; splatters ©mejnak/Shutterstock/HIP;
drips ©SergeyBitos/Shutterstock/HIP; JUSTICE poster ©Rrodrickbeiler/Dreamstime/HIP;
HOW MANY MORE poster ©Roman/Adobe Stock/HIP; STOP RACISM poster ©Roman
Chazov/Shutterstock/HIP
Figure 3.6: map of India ©Awesome_art_Creation/Shutterstock; apartment building
©JuliusKielaitis/Shutterstock; soda can ©avajjon/iStockphoto.com/HIP; DeLorean
©FlyingDoctor/Shutterstock
Page 72: ©North Wind Picture Archives/Alamy/HIP
Page 94: ©Everett Historical/Shutterstock/HIP
Figures 6.3 and 6.12: Rosie the Riveter, printed by permission of the Norman Rockwell Family
Agency, copyright ©1943 the Normal Rockwell Family Entities
Figure 7.9: map of Taiwan ©Peter Hermes Furian/Shutterstock; Taipei protest ©Pichi
Chuang/Reuters; Taiwan flag ©lmageClub/Getty Images/HIP; U.S.A. flag ©lmageClub/
Getty Images/HIP
Figure 7.14: flowers at far right ©Elizabeth Dowle/Quarto, Inc./Photodisc/Getty Images/
HIP
Page 140: Library of Congress/HIP
Page 141: ©Everett Collection Historical/Alamy/HIP
Page 142: ©Everett Collection Historical/Alamy/HIP